SOME CANADIAN GHOSTS

SOME CANADIAN
GHOSTS

Sheila Hervey

A POCKET BOOK EDITION published by
Simon & Schuster of Canada, Ltd. ∘ Markham, Ontario, Canada
Registered User of the Trademark

AN ORIGINAL CANADIAN

POCKET  BOOK

One of a series of Canadian books first published
by Simon & Schuster of Canada Limited
Jock Carroll, Editor

SOME CANADIAN GHOSTS

POCKET BOOK edition published April, 1973
5th printing........November, 1974

Cover design by John Richmond

This original POCKET BOOK edition is printed from brand-
new plates made from newly set, clear, easy-to-read type.
POCKET BOOK editions are published by POCKET BOOKS,
a division of Simon & Schuster of Canada, Ltd.,
330 Steelcase Road, Markham, Ontario L3R 2M1.
Trademarks registered in Canada and other countries.

+ Heraclitus (*circa*, 500 B.C.) "Because it is sometimes so unbelievable, the truth escapes becoming known."

— Robertson Davies *Fifth Business* "This monkeying with difficult, sacred things is a sure way to get yourself into a real old mess."

Acknowledgments

Many people helped me while I was writing this book. I would like to thank the following people for their stories, research, advice and encouragement; David L. Willford, Fort St. John, B.C.; Lauretta Kitchen, Teslin, Yukon; Sandy Wygle, Kindersley, Sask.; Mrs. E. Teslin, York University; Harold Weir, Vancouver, B.C.; Dr. Helen Creighton; Bill Bachop, Vancouver, B.C.; Robert Mainwaring, Brockville, Ont.; Jack Webster, Vancouver, B.C.; Leslie Holroyd, Vancouver, B.C.; John Plul, Vancouver, B.C.; Bill Bantey, Acton Vale; Arthur Dunn, Colgan, Ont.; Gordon L. Sculthorpe, Fort St. John; Al Forrest, Victoria, B.C.; Anne Dunlop, Mississauga, Ont.; Dr. D. Morganson, Waterloo, Ont. ; Mrs. Phyllis Barry, Caledon, Ont.; Pamela Ball and Murray Ball, Thornhill, Ont.; Nancy Carroll, Toronto, Ont.; Prudie Bond, Mississauga, Ont.; Elinor Belitsky, Mississauga, Ont.; F.E. Atkinson, Summerland, B.C.: Toy Carroll, Scarborough, Ont.; Reverend Tom Bartlett, Toronto and Joan Pelly of Mississauga.

CONTENTS

INTRODUCTION

Recently, the travel industry began to take an interest in the hitherto unexploited market of ghost-hunters. British Overseas Airways Corporation initiated the program. It offered a unique tour ; a package trip arranged to include an entire week of haunted houses in Great Britain. This tour, as it was advertized, included a varied selection of those private homes, estates and inns which are said to be consistently inhabited by spirits or ghosts. In each instance, the historical background surrounding and supposedly explaining the actual haunting was well-documented.

The airline made no guarantees. Still, there was a fair chance that any or all of the tour members might encounter supernatural manifestations or phenomena.

After reading about the projected British tour and realizing that I couldn't go quite that far to see a ghost, I sought an alternative. I began to wonder if there were ghosts closer to home. Were they truly a thing of the past, confined to faraway lands, or just a creation of ignorant superstition? Did we have some real ones of our very own right here in Canada just waiting to be discovered? Did the Eastern Maritime provinces have a virtual monopoly on spiritual manifestations, or could ghosts be found in areas representative of the entire country?

Hans Holzer is a popular writer dealing competently with contemporary ghosts. He contends that there are even more haunted houses in North America than in Great Britain. Where, then, are the haunting places of these elusive spectres? And, even more important, why is it that we so seldom hear about incidents involving the supernatural? If, as Holzer suggests, we do have all these ghosts, why is everyone so secretive about their presence in Canada? These were some of the questions that supplied me with the initial impetus to really start searching for Canadian ghosts. Once upon the quest, the sheer fascination of the material was enough to keep me hard at work.

Bluenose Ghosts (1957), by Dr. Helen Creighton, provided a good basic introduction to ghostly Canadiana and superstition. It soon became obvious that, other than the work of Dr. Creighton, very little serious research had been done upon the various evidences of the supernatural in Canada.

Some of the incidents in this book are taken from the library and research files of the newspapers published in those areas where the actual experiences took place. Others are totally new and come directly from people who were involved in unusual events not covered in any way by the various news media.

Dates and locations are as accurate as possible. The names of those involved are, for the most part, genuine. In a few cases, I have changed the names of individuals who felt, perhaps correctly, that they had experienced enough difficulty already. When small towns are involved, some names and sites have been omitted. This is deliberate. It is sometimes necessary to leave out pertinent details which might lead to too much neighborly curiosity.

The stories are as they happened; for the most part, the people involved are of secondary importance.

In recent years, ghost-hunting has been complicated by the increased ability of the average family to simply move away when it encounters a supernatural phenomenon. Many fascinating ghost stories of the nineteen-sixties end abruptly when the central family leaves the scene of physical disturbance in order to find a bit of peace and quiet. Fear is stronger than curiosity in this sort of situation. People pack up and run, sometimes with very little justification, rather than face that which they cannot understand.

In former times there was no such opportunity for escape. People derived their livelihood directly or indirectly from the land or sea. Their neighbors were not mere strangers; they were relatives, friends and allies in time of trouble. Moving in that period would have meant a serious economic, physical and emotional upheaval for such firmly-rooted families. It was something to be avoided at all costs.

Entire communities became involved in the local hauntings. The more knowledgeable and experienced individuals tried their various solutions, exorcisms and tactics against the unknown entity which had appeared in their midst. It is to their courage that we owe much of the material that today forms the backbone of our knowledge about psychic phenomena.

It is important to note that those afflicted with ghostly difficulties were not merely dismissed as "crack-pots". The communal effort to rid a family of an unwanted spirit indicates that ghosts were accepted as being very real, possibly dangerous, and a direct challenge to all concerned. Our ancestors did not flee; they fought.

Using newspaper reports and the statements of witnesses, I will try to recreate some of the more modern ghostly visitations and supernatural events that have occurred in Canada. You may well have had personal experiences that enable you to empathize with some of the people about whom you will be reading.

The incidents in this book are representative of almost all sections of the country. The final judgement as to their veracity will be dependent upon the open-mindedness and experience of the individual reader. Most of the foolish and unsupported cases have been eliminated in advance.

As we move along, I think you will come to agree with me on a number of basic points. Ghosts do exist and are very real to those who encounter them. We have with us representatives of the immediate past as well as those from the earliest days of Canada's history. Human experiences with supernatural phenomena are as common today as they were one hundred years ago.

In any collection of ghost stories there are generally a number of remarkably similar points when we compare the separate experiences. Some of the tales are almost identical in detail, although they may be poles apart in time and distance. This collection is no exception. There is a certain amount of overlapping of small detail. For example, the fact that animals can sense the arrival of a ghost is illustrated in several of the stories selected to show entirely different characteristics of the supernatural.

The term "supernatural" is a misnomer. It is employed throughout this book when the correct word should be "supernormal". Most of what we consider unnatural is merely that which we cannot fully understand. In a way, I am knowingly perpetuating an error, but the use of the popular term "supernatural" makes it easier for most readers.

Chapter One

A MOVEABLE GHOST

THE MAN WHO WALKED THROUGH MRS. STANDEN

Over the years countless people have reported seeing ghosts. These stories come from every country in the world and from every level of society. While a brush with the supernatural can be frightening it is still something you can tell your friends about if the conversation lags at the next party.

Traditionally, the average ghost haunts a particular place or area so that if you want to catch sight of it you can always visit the spot. On the other hand, if you want to avoid ghosts you can stay away from a place which has the reputation of being haunted.

But what if ghosts follow you from house to house?

For that kind of happening, involving three houses and nobody knows how many individual spirits, consider the strange story of Mrs. Pamela Ball of Willowdale, Ontario.

Pamela Ball is a petite, vivacious brunette in her middle years. She and her husband, Ray, came to Canada from England. He is a businessman, she works in a shopping plaza as a sales clerk. She has two teenage sons, Jonathan and Murray.

When you meet Mrs. Ball you do not think of her in connection with the supernatural. She is a bubbly person, outgoing, a good conversationalist. She takes a lively interest in her family and her work. She has never been connected with spiritualism in any way.

"Until these things began to happen to me, I wasn't the least bit interested in the supernatural." Mrs. Ball says now. "I still don't say I *believe* in ghosts. I'm not sure what I do believe."

In April, 1968, The Ball family moved into a farmhouse near Gormley, Ontario. Gormley is a hamlet just north of Toronto, a place which has almost been swallowed up by the expanding metropolis. But there are still some farms left in the area and the house rented by the Balls was quite ordinary.

It was a new frame construction built upon a century-old whitewashed brick foundation. There was nothing unusual about the house or the location.

The house was designed as a large T. The top of the T consisted of two bedrooms with a bathroom between them and a corridor running between each end. Mr. and Mrs. Ball occupied the bedroom at one end and just outside their door, in the hallway, was a closet.

The living room and kitchen area formed the stem of the letter T. The living room was a large rectangle with windows on three sides which meant it was bright in the day time but let in the flashes of passing car lights during the night. There was, in fact, so much light from traffic that it often illuminated the hallway outside Mrs. Ball's bedroom.

The other slight inconvenience was an extremely squeaky screen door on the outside of the main front door of the house. It was a thing the family often commented on. They always knew somebody had arrived even before they heard the knock because the screen had to be opened and it groaned like something from a horror show. These small things, which had no significance when they rented the house, became important later.

On the night Pamela Ball had her first taste of the unexplainable, she was sound asleep in her bedroom. The door to the hallway was open. From the bed, the hallway was clearly visible thanks to the sweeping of car lights from the highway.

Mrs. Ball was awakened from a deep sleep by three sharp knocks. Wondering who could possibly be calling in the middle of the night, she stared out into the hallway.

"I saw a brown, shapeless form hovering near the closet door. It had fluorescent quality. I was so terrified I woke up my husband. He saw the shape, too. But he hadn't heard the three knocks."

Ray Ball confirms this. As they stared at the strange shape, it disappeared through the closed door of the hall closet. Mrs. Ball was seized with a terrible, sudden chill. Ray had to massage her arms to restore circulation.

About three weeks after this first incident (which the Balls had pushed out of their minds), Ray and Pamela were dressing to go out for the evening. Both heard three sharp knocks.

"It must be the paper man." Pamela said to her husband. "But it isn't his night to collect."

Both husband and wife thought it odd that they had not heard the noisy screen door opening to allow the person to knock on the inside door. Pamela Ball went to the door but there was nobody there.

She was puzzled enough by these two incidents to make enquiries from the couple who had previously rented the house. They told her that they'd often been disturbed by unexplained raps on the front door. Next, Mrs. Ball asked her mother, Mrs. Lilian Standen, if she had ever noticed anything strange about the house when she had stayed over as a guest.

It appeared that Mrs. Standen certainly had. But she had not wanted to mention it to her daughter. On an earlier visit, Mrs. Standen had been sleeping in an upstairs bedroom of the house. Something woke her in the middle of the night. Without opening her eyes, Mrs. Standen says she *knew* there was a man standing at the foot of her bed. A feeling of icy cold came over her and she had the frightening sensation that the man was trying, (in Mrs. Standen's words) "to walk right through me." The idea came into her mind that if the man succeeded in touching her heart, she would die. After that, she refused to sleep upstairs and if she was staying over, slept in the living room downstairs.

The Ball family were sufficiently curious to try to find out something about the house as it had been in earlier days. Since the foundation was still there, they reasoned that there might be some connection between the old house and the things happening in the new one.

"We tried to trace the history of the old house, but all we found out was that it had burned down. The ruins fell into the foundations, somebody told us. But nobody actually knew whether any person was killed or injured in the fire."

So that seemed to end the mystery. The Ball family dismissed the problem and in August, 1969, they moved to another rented farmhouse near Buttonville, Ontario.

THE TERRIBLE DOLL

Buttonville is also a small village north of Toronto and not too far from Gormley. It is one of the older settlements in the province and the farmhouse which the Balls now occupied was built around 1830.

This house was large, with Gothic-style windows, a workable fireplace, an unusual front porch roof fashioned of bentwood, and a musty basement which nobody liked to enter. It had a center hall plan with a staircase to the second floor. For some reason, the front door and the porch were never used. A back door was used instead.

The Buttonville farmhouse sits on fifty acres. It is reached by a long, dark avenue of ancient pine trees. From the beginning, the Ball family felt that the driveway was a bit intimidating. It was especially gloomy at night.

The second floor of the house was only partially divided into bedrooms. On one side, above the living room, were two large bedrooms. The Balls occupied the front one, and the two boys, Jonathan and Murray, took the back one. The other half of the second floor was one large, open space but still useable for guests.

When they rented the house, Pamela and Ray were pleased. It was large. They liked the space, and the design. Murray Ball, 17, was especially pleased because he had been collecting small antiques for a couple of years and this was a perfect setting for them.

Murray remembers the first day the family moved in.

"I liked the house but the day started off in a kind of weird way." Murray recalls, "This neighbor from down the road, Marion Johns, happened to arrive while we were still putting in the furniture. She's psychic. I wanted to take her upstairs to show her some of my antiques, my bottles, and coins and stamps. But she refused to go upstairs with me."

Mrs. Johns announced that she didn't feel good about the house, particularly about the stairs. Murray coaxed her to accompany him up to the second floor but she wouldn't stay.

"I don't like it up here. In fact, I don't like this house." Mrs. Johns said positively.

Murray still felt good about the house but he was surprised at his neighbor's attitude. She accompanied him to the living room. Here she announced that she could see an elderly couple sitting near the fireplace. There had been terrible arguments, a lot of strife in the house, Mrs. Johns said.

Murray decided not to take too much notice of this. He felt that perhaps the Ball family would change the whole atmosphere of the place. They were a happy, agreeable group and with different people, furniture, the house would be fine.

It was six months before Murray, or any of the family thought again of the dismal mood of the house.

In May, 1970 (Murray later checked the date and found that it had been the full moon, but he did not know this when the event occurred) the next nerve-shattering act took place.

This occurrence was connected with an antique doll. During the winter Murray had become friendly with a teenage boy who lived in an old house across the street. Tom Harwood (not his real name) not only lived in a Victorian-style house, but in a rather old-fashioned way. It was as if the clock had been turned back. The furniture, the ornaments, even the conversation in the Harwood house was out-of-date.

Tom lived with his father. Both the grandmother and mother had died within the same week in the house. Tom and Mr. Harwood behaved as if they were still alive.

"They talked as if the two women were still alive. It was like walking into a movie set, with everything going on in some other age. I even found two enormous old hatpins sticking in a pincushion in the bathroom." Murray says, describing his visits to the Harwood house.

Despite the oddity of the situation, Murray was enchanted. He loved the antique furniture, the memorabilia, the photographs, the books, the wild assortment of leftovers from a bygone day. He had begun to trade coins with Tom for some of the smaller family pieces. One of the things he acquired in this way was an old doll.

The doll was lying on the floor of a bedroom closet. Tom said it had belonged first to his grandmother and then later to his mother. Since both women were gone, the doll was discarded.

"I never did *like* the doll." Murray explains. "But I knew it was old and probably quite valuable. It was a depressing doll, really. I couldn't imagine a child liking it or wanting to hold it."

The doll's body was made in a primitive way; dirty brown cotton stuffed with straw. The head and hands were bisque, a dull-finish china popular in the 19th century. It was meant to be a baby doll but the face was somehow unhappy and pouty. The painted, faded blue eyes were distinctly unpleasant. The hair had been painted on over a slightly raised configuration in the china. Altogether, it wasn't much as an ornament but Murray took the doll home and placed it on the mantel in the living room along with a pair of high-button shoes.

The doll had been in the house about a week when it asserted its personality. The evening is indelibly impressed upon Murray's mind.

On the evening in question, Murray and Jonathan had invited two friends over to play cards. Ray and Pamela Ball had gone out for the evening. When the card game broke up, late in the evening, the four boys left the dining room table and went to the living room to sit about and chat. The two guests, Dave McNally and Bill Johns, became fascinated with the doll.

When Murray describes that night he says, "I couldn't figure out why they both suddenly took an interest in the doll. They'd both seen it before. But Bill said he didn't like the doll and Dave said he didn't like it either. I was amazed. Still, I like to talk about my antiques to anybody who will listen."

Murray crossed the room to pick up the doll, but as he reached toward it, his hand was pushed back by an unseen force. Both Dave and Bill say they clearly remember seeing Murray's hand thrust back. All four boys were both surprised and frightened.

At this point Murray felt intensely cold. His flesh was covered with goose bumps and he felt what might be described as an electric current pass through him. His hair stood on end, just as he had read in books and stories. His friends saw his reaction. The boys say that they 'felt something in the room'. Murray was shaking. He was very upset.

"We're getting out of this house." Dave said.

The four boys ran toward the door. Murray was last and he had the definite feeling that he couldn't go through the door and out of the house. Something, he didn't know what, seemed to be forcing him to stay in the house.

"Something was telling me to stay. I heard Dave say, 'Come on, don't be silly, Murray', but I kept saying 'I'm not going out'."

One of the boys yanked Murray by the arm, forcibly removing him from the house. Once he was clear of the house, Murray no longer felt the power pulling him. He was, however, ice cold and still shaking.

The boys walked down the road to the home of Bill Johns. They told Mrs. Johns about their experience and she suggested that Murray and Jonathan spend the night there. They telephoned their parents and described to them what had occurred. Because of the incident, nobody slept in the Ball house that night, the Balls electing to stay with their friends.

The next day Ray Ball picked up the doll, took it from the mantel and placed it in an old shed quite far from the house. It lay there in the shed for several days and was, in fact, still lying in the shed when Mrs. Ball had her next weird experience with the supernatural.

About a week after the doll had been removed, Mrs. Ball woke early in the morning. The house was empty except for herself and her dog, Tracy. On that beautiful May morning she was thinking of picking rhubarb from the garden to make a pie. One could scarcely imagine a topic less likely to produce a spirit.

In the midst of her thoughts about rhubarb pie, Pamela Ball felt the bed vibrating. Thinking Tracy was scratching, she decided to push the dog off the foot of the bed. Instead of accomplishing that, Mrs. Ball felt a force pushing *her*. From beneath her shoulder blades, something was trying to push her from the bed toward the high, narrow window which overlooked the front porch. She saw herself going out of the window feet first and then slithering to the ground from the porch.

"All I could think of was that 'it' wanted me out of the house." Mrs. Ball remembers now. She didn't know what she meant by 'it' and she felt a tingling sensation as if an electric current had run through her. Following that, a feeling of profound evil swept over her.

"Before I felt that, I didn't have any idea what evil meant. I'd never really thought about the meaning of the word."

All she wanted now was to get out of the house. But at the same time she was desperately afraid to go down the stairs. It seemed to her that the force which she had felt pushing her toward the window might push her down the stairs. So she sat down, in the bright morning sunshine, and bumped her way down the stairs to the bottom like a child. She was standing out in the garden when her husband came home from work unexpectedly. He was astonished to see her standing outside doing nothing. She told him about the force in the bedroom, but he could find no explanation for it.

The 'presence' in the house made itself felt again within a few days, this time in a more homey way. (Or perhaps it was another presence and not the same one which had tried to push Pamela Ball out of the window). This time it was seven o'clock in the evening and Pamela and her son, Jonathan were together in the living room.

"Somebody's baking an apple pie." Jonathan said, suddenly. "Is there somebody else home?"

"There's nobody home but us. I smell it too. Like cooking apples and cinnamon. The cinnamon is strong." Mrs. Ball agreed.

It was a delicious odor and it seemed to come from the old basement. Since that idea was utterly ridiculous the two went to the kitchen. There was nobody baking an apple pie. They next thought the smell might be coming from outside. Outside the house there was absolutely no smell of baking cinnamon. Trying hard to find some explanation, Mrs. Ball recalled that one of Murray's antiques was a small tin which had once held cinnamon. But when they located it, the tin was in Murray's room and the lid was firmly on.

Later that same evening, not having heard about his wife's earlier experience, Ray Ball came home and sat alone in the living room. He distinctly smelled cooking cinnamon coming from the basement.

The doll was eventually given to a doll collector and no more has been heard about it.

These were the most striking incidents in the Buttonville house. But the entire time the Ball family lived there they heard footsteps where nobody was walking. Unexplained and coming at unusual times, the footsteps took different forms. They did not always come from the same location. Almost every visitor to the house, and all family members had some experience with peculiar footsteps.

A GENTLE SIGH

For example, Mrs. Standen (Mrs. Ball's mother) was sleeping in the open area on the second floor one night when both Jonathan and Murray were out. Late at night she thought she heard Jonathan coming in. At any rate, she heard footsteps running up the stairs, then the sound of a body sinking onto a bed followed by a gentle sigh. In the morning she commented to Pamela Ball,

"Jonathan was very late last night."

"Yes, he was." Pamela said, because she too had wakened to hear the running footsteps. Both women went to the boys' bedroom to call Jonathan for breakfast but he wasn't there. The bed had not been slept in.

Because they lived in the country, the house was often filled with overnight guests. Many of the guests reported footsteps and the sound of whistling when there was nobody about to make them.

Ken Farr, one of Murray's boy friends, recalls staying overnight with Murray and having what he calls a 'peculiar experience'. In the morning both boys were ready to go down for breakfast and Ken followed Murray out of the bedroom and toward the staircase.

"I was right behind him. About two steps. Yet when I reached the top of the stairs, Murray was out of sight. It just wasn't possible."

In April, 1972, the Ball family moved from the Buttonville house to a town house in Willowdale. They did not move because of the disturbances (most of the time they ignored them) but because it was a hard house to heat. Mrs. Ball always felt cold in the house and did not want to face another winter there.

Two days before they were due to move, however, Mrs. Ball awoke in the middle of the night to the same tingling sensation she'd felt before. Then she felt icy cold. A voice, as if from inside her head kept repeating, "I'm dead". Mrs. Ball felt sure that the voice didn't mean that

Mrs. Ball herself was dead, but rather it was talking about somebody else. The voice was neither a man's voice nor a woman's.

On the day they moved, the Balls were relieved to think that they would be finished with the series of inexplicable happenings. They had no real desire to delve into the supernatural. Any inquiries they'd made were because of natural curiosity. They looked forward to the new town house, the new location. The past would be past. Or so they thought.

Nothing less 'haunted' than the town house can be imagined. It is almost new, contemporary in design and has several levels each joined by a short flight of stairs. There is a fresh, light feeling about the place.

I WANT OUT!

Despite this, Mrs. Ball had a new fright only five months after she moved into the Willowdale house. It began with a dream. She was back in Buttonville and running up the dark, windy driveway with its shadowy pines, toward the house.

Suddenly, as so often happens in dreams, she was in the old basement (a place the family had always avoided when they actually lived there) and seeing once again the cupboards on the walls. She smelled again the unpleasant, musty odor of the place and felt the pall of the tiny, dark rooms. A loud banging upstairs drew her attention to the living room door. She went toward it and found herself at the foot of the main staircase.

"I recognized the bannister." Mrs Ball says, "because the yellow paint was all worn through. I could hear a woman shouting from beneath the stairs, 'I want out!' I knew it was that 'presence' again. I was absolutely terrified and woke up. As soon as I was awake I was freezing and I had to wake Ray to massage my arms."

Two nights after this nightmare occurred, she woke

again in the middle of the night. She felt uneasy, although she could not think of any real reason why she should. At this time, Murray was away, and she walked down the short flight of stairs which led to both his bedroom and the bathroom. She had been keeping the bedroom door closed but saw that it was open.

Because the door sticks and could not have swung open by itself, she felt there was something odd about it being open. She took hold of the doorhandle to pull it shut. The familiar smell of the musty basement of the Buttonville house came to her from Murray's bedroom. As she tried to shut the door, a force on the other side pulled against her. She could not close the door, no matter how she tried.

"I felt the 'presence' was there. In this new house. And that if I went into Murray's room I'd come face to face with it. The idea was so revolting that I let go of the door handle. Tracy was with me, and she growled and her hair stood up. I was terrified."

Finally, she went back to bed. In the morning the bedroom door was still open but there was no longer a feeling of evil. The musty odor was gone.

At this time, Mrs. Ball has no idea whether or not she has had her last experience with the 'presence'. She does not know what it wants her to do, if anything, and why it seems to have followed her from the Buttonville house. There is no way of knowing whether the 'thing' in the Gormley house followed her to Buttonville, and then to Willowdale. Or whether each spirit is a separate entity.

At one time, the Ball family theorized that the 'presence' may have accompanied some of the antiques from the Harwood house across the road. The doll, for example, belonged to both the women who died in that house during a single week. The Gormley incident is entirely separate, if one takes this view.

The doll, being the most vivid single incident, does make a strong case for that theory. But Mrs. Johns 'saw' strife and an elderly couple in the Buttonville house and the associations with a voice under the staircase seem to indicate that there was something in the Buttonville house itself quite independent of the doll. The doll may have been used as a focus for forces already in the house.

A theory which would embrace all three houses is that Pamela Ball is the attraction. That she is super-sensitive to any spirits which happen to be around and that they are able, somehow, to tune in to her. The idea is not new, of course. Many psychics have this experience; if there's a ghost around, they see it or hear it or feel it.

In her autobiography, "Portrait of My Victorian Youth", Alice Pollock tells of her encounters with ghosts in a matter-of-fact way.

She saw her first ghost in her own parish church and later found out that a skeleton had been found in the wall behind the place where she had seen the shadowy form. Friends sometimes asked her to psychometrize houses and she was able to do so on more than one occasion. Past events would appear to her, usually scenes of tragedy, which would explain some haunting which had been making life uncomfortable. In Leeds Castle, which happened to belong to a relative, Mrs. Pollock saw a ghost which was probably Queen Joan of Navarre. She often used the crystal to see into the future. And this was a very proper lady from a wealthy and well-connected English family.

Another Englishwoman, Joan Grant, is one of the most famous contemporary psychics alive today. If there is a ghost or spirit in the vicinity, Joan Grant will see it. In her books she tells of visions of the past, the future, and of various encounters with the spirits of the dead.

It is possible, then, that Pamela Ball is 'open' to communication with some spirits and that is why she has had supernatural experiences in all three houses.

Chapter Two

WEST COAST SPIRITS

WALDO

Living with a ghost in a castle or a quaint old mansion is one thing; sharing accommodations with one in a small residence is another. It can become unbearably overcrowded.

That's what painter Eric Henderson and his wife found out in the memorable summer of 1957. Eric (not his real name) thought he'd struck a fine bargain indeed when he rented a small furnished house in the village of Waldo, in northwestern British Columbia, for twenty-five dollars a month. Even as far back as 1957, this was considered a most reasonable rent.

"The house had two bedrooms," Eric Henderson says, "but both my wife and I had an uncomfortable feeling in one of them. I can't explain it even today. But we decided not to use that bedroom."

The house was well kept up and fully furnished. There were gaily colored curtains at the windows, a wide selection of books on the shelves and even a piano. A disembowelled but finely polished grandfather clock stood near the front door. The house was in a convenient location, too, right next to the public school. For this reason, it had often been rented to schoolteachers during the term months.

Eric Henderson came down from Fort St. John where he had been painting. He was so pleased with the house that he took it for the two summer months. Eric had heard vague rumors around the village that the house was haunted, but he dismissed this idea as mere nonsense. Anyway, at the asking price, the house was worth taking some risks. Besides, fishing in the area was just too good to forfeit over a ghost.

From the moment the Hendersons moved in, however, until the day they left to return to Fort St. John, the house lived up to its reputation. It provided a series of peculiar happenings for the new tenants.

The trouble usually began about ten-thirty in the evening. The grandfather clock would strike despite the fact that it lacked crucial internal machinery. But strike it did, every evening, in defiance of basic mechanical principle and theory.

This was often followed by the determined closing of some of the doors inside the house. The Hendersons could see them closing slowly, dragging across the floor but there wasn't a soul touching them.

This was all the more curious because only the bathroom door and the door of the unused bedroom moved. Those doors were too heavy to have been closed by a draft even if there had been one in the house. Occasionally windows would be raised and then dropped with an ear-splitting crash. An unseen force would flip through the pages of books left lying about the room. And, for an unusual touch, fishing rod reels spun of their own accord until the lines were hopelessly entangled.

Although there was nothing exactly evil or dangerous about the manifestations, they did tend to make life a little upsetting. So Eric Henderson decided to do a bit of checking. Perhaps, he thought, someone was playing a practical joke on him. Or there might be some natural explanation for the odd happenings.

"Both my wife and I checked the house thoroughly. It seemed to be structurally sound," Henderson recalls, "But sometimes tremors are blamed for door-closing and window-rattling. We wanted to make sure that wasn't the problem. But nobody in the neighborhood was using explosives and there were no reports of earthquakes. We agreed not to touch the objects being moved about, but still they moved by themselves. Books, papers and fishing gear were never the way we left them."

Mrs. Henderson believed that the ghost was looking for something in the books. It was most persistent in its attention to them.

The local postmistress told the Hendersons that the ghost was reputed to be that of an older man who had died in the house many years before.

"In the bedroom we didn't use." Henderson says with awe.

The Hendersons hung onto the house until fall, still not any closer to solving the mystery of their invisible guest. Then they moved out to make room for a pair of young married school teachers.

The newcomers evidently didn't know anything about the reputation of the house and did not mix with the local people. Since they were planning to stay for some time, they rearranged the furniture, including the books, to suit themselves.

When the new couple moved in, the townsfolk watched and waited. Not long after, the piano began to play at three o'clock in the morning. There was no one near it. The young wife ran screaming into the street crying that the house was haunted. She was quite appalled when the neighbors, aroused by the noise, assured her that it was. They already knew.

The couple refused to return to the house despite the hour. They found other, more orthodox, accommodations a little farther from the school. Unlike the Hendersons, the school teachers were not prepared to cope with a resident-ghost in return for any reduction in their monthly rental.

Although nobody saw the ghost in Waldo, there was no doubt in the minds of the tenants, and of some of the townspeople that some sort of spirit lived there. Too many peculiar and unnatural things were going on in that house. The general concensus was evidently shared by the owner who continued to ask a ridiculously low rental.

THE ROSEWOOD BED

It is not often that a single, powerful manifestation takes place and then entirely disappears. In Vancouver, however, there were a dozen witnesses to a bizarre scene which dissolved a jolly party and caused a young couple to sell their house immediately.

The house in this story has since been levelled. The people who saw the 'vision' are now free to talk, although fear and shock kept them quiet for many years. The tale can be added to the ghostly folklore of Canada.

During the early 1930's, a middle-aged man and his slightly older wife moved into the Vancouver area. They built a large modern house in the West End. The woman was friendly and outgoing but her husband was not interested in making friends. He took pains to make it quite clear that he wished to be left alone. He refused all invitations without explanation, and did not issue any to the neighbors.

The couple lived in the house for about six months. Then the wife suddenly became very ill and died almost immediately. The husband informed the local doctor who attended that his wife had an existing heart condition and a coronary attack was certified as the cause of death.

The husband lost no time in selling the big house and moving away from the district. If they thought about it at all, the neighbors put this action down to the sorrow of a man who had just lost his wife. However, they were slightly puzzled when he firmly refused to leave a forwarding address.

A young married couple bought the house and though they had liked it immensely in the beginning, they soon began to sense something unusual about the atmosphere of the place.

Since these people were completely unfamiliar with any kind of psychic phenomena, they could not explain why they felt so uneasy in their lovely new home. They couldn't settle down and found themselves particularly uncomfortable in the large room on the main floor which had formerly been used as the master bedroom.

They decided to remodel the entire house from top to the bottom, blaming the feeling they had on the decor. It was a massive and very expensive assignment for such a young couple. They undertook to knock out walls to enlarge the drawing room area which included the bedroom they didn't like. By increasing the area, they hoped to reduce the discomfort. Furniture, rugs, walls, all were completely changed. Only the outside structure remained the same.

When the renovations were finally complete, the young couple decided to hold a housewarming party. They wanted to celebrate their apparent success in removing all signs of the former owners. Six couples, all close friends, were invited and until midnight the party appeared to be a great success. There was no hint of trouble.

In the midst of all this gaiety, an icy chill descended upon the large room. No one spoke, or moved. The attention of all the guests was somehow rivetted on the far end of the drawing room where the master bedroom had once been situated.

Suddenly, the vision of a large rosewood four-poster appeared. On the massive bed lay a woman who was obviously very near death. She stared in terror at the man sitting beside the bed. The man wore a small, self-satisfied smile.

"That's the man who built the house!" One of the house guests exclaimed. "And that's his wife. She died here in the house. But why is she looking at him like that?"

"That's where the master bedroom was." The young wife whispered, "We didn't like the room, so we took out the wall."

The vision faded as silently as it had appeared.

Afraid of being accused of over-drinking, or over-imagination or both, the guests pledged themselves to strict secrecy. They would tell no one, they agreed, about what had happened.

Oddly enough, nobody seems to have thought of informing the local police so the matter could be investigated. But then, who would have believed the story? Psychic phenomena were seldom mentioned in those days.

The house was resold immediately. The buyers were not told about the peculiar atmosphere; nor was the apparition discussed. All the lovely new furnishings were turned over to an auction house for prompt disposal.

One of the guests from the ill-fated party was a little braver or a little more curious than the rest. She went to the auction sale. She saw the new carpet from the drawing room, a carpet laid down just before the party.

There were four deep, clear indentations; as if a large, heavy object had been sitting on it.

The woman took the trouble to examine the four depressions. She could scarcely believe her eyes. They formed a large, perfect rectangle — a rectangle about the size of a large four-poster. It was almost as if the massive bed from the apparition had been real enough and heavy enough to leave permanent markings in the new material.

After the house was resold there were no further reports of the apparition. The new owners experienced no difficulty. It was as if the single, powerful apparition had used all the energy available to impress itself upon the party-goers. Today, a large apartment block stands on the site of this experience and only two of the guests are alive to confirm the story. One of them is the woman who attended the auction sale. She has no explanation for the incident, but merely reports it as it happened.

THE PAINTING THAT CHANGED

Well-meaning and genuinely interested individuals sometimes thoroughly confuse the detailed investigation of a supernatural manifestation. These people, upon learning about a reported haunting in their area, immediately begin to gather at the scene. They turn up in incredible numbers. They mean no harm, and want only to satisfy their curiosity. But, their mere presence hinders relaxed interviews and prevents the necessary examination of the property involved.

The following case is an example of this increasingly popular desire to learn all about unnatural events and, perhaps, to believe in the existence of ghosts.

Chilliwack, British Columbia, is a small (population 8,681) town situated about 100 miles from Vancouver in the lower Fraser Valley. The area is noted mainly for its high agricultural development, specifically cattle and an impressive production of hops, raspberries, beans, peas and corn. It is not noted for an interest in psychic phenomena.

However, in December of 1965, Douglas and Hetty Frederickson bought a twelve-room house on Williams Street North in Chilliwack. The town and the Fredericksons were catapulted into an unnerving experience which finally forced Douglas and Hetty to move to Sayward on Vancouver Island.

Hetty Frederickson had a series of vivid and recurrent nightmares about the body of a woman lying on the floor in a hallway. It was not a hallway, or area which she recognized in the house.

Describing the woman in her dreams, Hetty reported, "She wears a red dress covered with yellow flowers, and her face is terrified."

The nightmares were followed by odd things happening in the daylight, too. One of the upstairs bedrooms was unused but furnished. For some peculiar reason, the bureau drawers there kept opening and shutting when the room was quite empty. An old bedstead moved mysteriously from one place to another.

Mrs. Frederickson was not easily frightened. She determined to find out what going on in her home. She sat up in the empty bedroom with a candle for three nights in a row hoping to get a glimpse of the intruder. On the third night, she saw what appeared to be a misty figure standing by the window. The shape, however, was too vague to allow her to compare it with the woman in her dreams.

Hetty was an artist. Born in Indonesia she later spent three years at the Academy of Creative Arts in The Hague. She was curious and anxious to put her talent to work to solve the mystery of the house.

She would paint the woman she saw in her dreams.

In May, 1966, Hetty began to sketch an impression of the elusive woman. She thought that the sketch might help her to identify the individual behind all the strange happenings.

But Mrs. Frederickson was in for yet another shock.

"The woman's face kept changing into that of a man. I didn't touch the painting but it gradually changed. It's all very disturbing."

If Hetty had ever read *The Secret of Dorian Grey*, or seen the movie based upon the book, she would have known that there is a fictional precedent for a portrait that alters by itself. But the apparent change of sex was a most unusual development. The Fredericksons began to wonder if their ghost might be a male struggling to communicate with them. Or, perhaps there might even be two ghosts.

Finally Mrs. Frederickson finished her portrait, but she was not satisfied with the results.

"Sketching the woman was not easy. Everytime I tried to paint, the face would start out as a man even as I tried to paint a woman. But I really concentrated and at last painted a likeness of the woman. Now something is altering it into a man again."

Now the excitement began in earnest. Reporters and neighbors tried to find out about previous owners of the big house. But this was really a hopeless task. It had been used as a boardinghouse and the turnover of people was such that it was almost impossible to trace a history. A few former occupants did telephone the Fredericksons to tell of secrets chutes which were alleged to run from the top of the house to the bottom. Nobody could locate these chutes, however.

Meanwhile, the haunting continued. It was discovered that a man had committed suicide in the house ten years earlier.

Another, more fanciful story had a woman killed in the house and cemented into a chimney. The Fredericksons felt, perhaps correctly, that a fertile imagination had started this latter tale. The press had, by this time, reported Hetty's nightmares about a woman. It seemed logical that someone might have been trying to provide a colorful explanation.

In June of 1966, Professor Geoffrey Riddehough, a member of the Psychical Research Society of England was conducting Classics lectures at the University of British Columbia. He was consulted about the Frederickson haunting.

Professor Riddehough made what seemed to be a rather brief study of the case. When questioned by members of the press and radio he refused to make a statement. He said, though, that he planned to write a paper on the matter.

No real help seemed to be forthcoming as far as the Fredericksons were concerned.

"The face is changing all the time." Hetty said about her painting, "It looks as if it's moving."

She threatened to move the painting right out of the house if it kept changing.

It was decided to investigate the house more carefully. This led to some rather strange discoveries. There was a door hidden behind some old panelling. It led into the bedroom where so many of the odd noises were heard and where the furniture had a predilection for moving by itself. The opening was right beside the old bedstead which had caused so much confusion earlier in the haunting.

Another passage was found leading to a turret at the top of the house. But there was nothing there except the usual insulation materials.

The searchers then reached the attic. Hetty said this was the location of the body in her dreams. This was where the terrified woman had been lying. The surrounding area was exactly like that of her dreams.

Since the press were in on the hauntings, people began to treat the house as a tourist site. They turned up in droves. One Sunday seven hundred visitors showed up, hoping to view the secret passages and catch a quick look at Hetty's ghost.

Shortly after this, the Fredericksons decided that they would have to move. They could not seem to solve the mystery; nor could they endure the stream of traffic and the avalanche of telephone calls asking for the latest news. They moved to Sayward, which is a small logging community about two hundred and fifty miles north of Victoria, British Columbia. Mr. Frederickson is a logger and Hetty now teaches art.

The house stood empty for some time, the target of vandals. In 1968 a group of young musicians moved into the house, cleaned up the property, mended the fences and fixed up the trampled flower beds. There were no further sightings of the ghost, although the house still belonged to the Fredericksons at that time.

And what about the painting done by Hetty at the height of the haunting?

The painting was donated by Mrs. Frederickson five years ago to the Haunted House exhibit of Station CKNW in Vancouver. They were running the display to raise money for their Orphans' Fund. The painting is now on loan to a Japanese exhibition.

Despite Mrs. Frederickson's claims about the painting turning into a portrait of a man, the case seems somewhat different. John Plul, promotion manager of the Vancouver radio station says that the picture clearly shows a woman.

"The painting is about eight feet high by five feet wide. Done mainly in oranges and blacks, it is of a woman looking through a bedroom window. She has her arms folded. Her left eye and the left side of her face are painted in but there is nothing on the right side of her face."

According to Mr. Plul, the painting shows Mrs. Frederickson's version of the face. The right side was supposed to have filled in by itself during the haunting.

Some tests were made on the right side of the face

and indicated that there was no paint pigment. It has been "worn down" by people rubbing their fingers on it to test for pigment.

John Plul firmly believes Mrs. Frederickson was sincere about her dream.

At the time of the Frederickson haunting, many people said that there was absolutely nothing the matter with the Chilliwack house. In retrospect, it would appear that they were wrong. Even though there are some things about Mrs. Frederickson's story that seem a bit odd, a new group of people are now experiencing trouble in the same house. Similarities between the two situations are apparent. Nightmares occur in both stories and other details of the two hauntings are comparable.

In the spring of 1972, a new family bought the controversial Chilliwack residence and almost immediately began to have difficulty. The present owners do not believe in ghosts; with eight children they have more than enough live activity to keep them busy. But they have been forced to admit that there is something most peculiar about the large house.

Several of the young children have begun to have nightmares, much like the ones that frightened Mrs. Frederickson so badly. Doors bang for no apparent reason and the family dog, normally quite fearless, has been found cowering and whimpering with fear in a corner.

For some unexplained reason, the new owners are afraid of going into the basement at night. This fear was quite pronounced when they first moved in during the spring and it lessened during the summer months. But, with the approach of winter, the banging of doors began again and the basement area regained its frightening atmosphere.

The present owners believe that there are three separate ghosts sharing the building with them. There is a female ghost who has been blamed for moving the thermostat up to 80 degrees on several occasions. The presence of this ghost is also felt by the family when they are watching television late at night.

Then there is another spectre, a male who seems to have a child-like mind (perhaps the result of mongolism) who seems responsible for the door-banging sessions in the early morning hours.

The last ghost is perhaps the most disturbing of the spirits. It apparently has a feeling that is very different from the doorbanger and the television-watcher. This spirit has badly frightened several members of the family who have encountered it in darkened hallways. According to the lady of the house, people who meet this last ghost experience a cold chill on their backs and are unable to move for several long minutes.

Usually men are skeptical of hauntings. The man who heads up the large family in Chilliwack is no exception; he does not believe in ghost stories. For this reason, it is even more impressive that he has slept for several nights with a gun beneath his pillow.

There are still no satisfactory explanations for the hauntings in Chilliwack; perhaps there never will be.

GOOD SCOTCH AND A LITTLE LOVE

A missing bottle of scotch, a messed-up bed, a travelling chef and an incredulous policeman are not the most common ingredients for a ghost story. But in Vancouver, there was a case involving all four of these elements.

In September, 1968, Diane Dunsmore, Cathy Sheppard and Marie Simpson, rented a small part of an old house on West Eleventh Street in Vancouver. Two of the girls were attending university and the third was hunting for a job.

At first, the girls were not aware of anything unusual about the house. Then they began to hear the sound of furniture being shifted about during the night. They heard footsteps echoing in the empty part of the house when nobody else was home.

Their landlord, a man called Ferdinand Santarpia, was away a lot, He was, according to the accounts a 'travelling chef.' In October Mr. Santarpia returned from a short trip to find that someone had broken into his bedroom in the basement apartment during his absence.

A half bottle of scotch was missing and someone had moved a candy jar from its proper position. The police found evidence of a tussle on Mr. Santarpia's bed.

Constable W.H. Campbell was the investigating officer. To him, Mr. Santarpia made it quite plain that he thought his young roomers might have forced entry into his apartment, made off with his liquor and used his bed. The girls had told the policeman about their 'ghost'. Mr. Santarpia was furious.

"I've been in this house five years and I've never heard or seen any ghosts. That's nonsense about a ghost. Whoever heard of a ghost that drinks scotch and smooches ?"

Nobody had.

It is natural to suspect the girls of using the ghost story to cover their own participation in the basement break-in. Or it *would* be except for a few facts that tend to support their story. They had already discussed the strange noises with a psychologist at the University of British Columbia prior to the theft incident.

And Diane claimed, "We made a Ouija board and got some very funny results."

Diane did not explain what kind of results might have indicated a scotch-drinking ghost, but the spirit was obviously very real to the girls — as real to them as it was unreal to their unhappy landlord.

As for Constable Campbell, he reported that the girls were serious about the ghost and badly frightened. One of them even broke into tears. He stated.

"I can't tell you whether or not they are imagining things or if someone is playing practical jokes or what, but anyway the suite was entered and the goods stolen."

At last report, Mr. Santarpia was adamant.

"It's ridiculous nonsense, and I don't want to talk about it anymore!"

LADY BY THE SEA

Sometimes ghost-watching is an acceptable community sport. This is the case, evidently, at Oak Bay on the British Columbia coastline.

Every spring an entire community of ghosts appears. They gather on the rocky, jutting point of land that runs out into the sea at Oak Bay. Local residents congregate to watch from a safe and respectable distance. When the sea is calm, distinct voices from the past can be heard by those who listen on the shoreline.

Many ghostly figures are reported to appear at Oak Bay but a single spirit, that of a lone woman, stands apart. There is a story involving a woman killed by her husband at this place in 1936. He later killed himself and his body was found floating in a nearby bed of kelp. Who the rest of the group are, nobody can determine. They come, and they are there, and that's all that can be said definitely.

While the ghost community is often seen by a number of people together, a more unusual sighting was reported in 1964 by two teenagers. The boy, Anthony Gregson, was then sixteen years old. He was strolling on a seaside golf course with a girl friend shortly after nine o'clock in the evening. It was early April, the usual time for the first visitation of Oak Bay ghosts. And the Victoria Golf Course, where the couple was walking, is frequently used by those who wish to observe the returning spirits.

Gregson was described by his principal as an unimaginative and honest young man. He made good grades in the eleventh grade at Oak Bay High School. His companion refused to make a statement but did back up the one made by Anthony.

"I don't wish to become involved." She said.

Anthony tells the story this way:

"We were joking about ghosts for awhile and suddenly we became very serious. At first, we didn't see anything but we could feel a definite change in the atmosphere. Then we saw her! She was about a thousand yards away and appeared to be running over the stones on the beach without touching them. I assumed it was a woman because she appeared to have a dress on. She was a luminous gray with an aura about her. When she reached the furthermost point of land, she stopped and looked out to sea as if she were expecting someone. I would rather like to think she was."

Anthony asked his companion for assurance. She agreed that she saw the woman, too.

"We must have watched her for about five minutes and my friend assured me that I wasn't seeing things. The ghost moved with much more ease than a human and had a certain grace of action, especially in her arms. Other features were less distinct."

Gregson and his companion left without waiting to see how long the ghost woman would remain by the shore. So there is no way of knowing if another spirit joined the first one as she seemed to expect. Perhaps the teenagers felt that they might be intruding upon very personal matters. It is also possible that they were somewhat frightened.

Up to this point Gregson had declared himself to be openminded on the subject of ghosts. Living in a community where ghosts are accepted by a large number of people, it is likely that he had heard many stories about the various manifestations. But, until that spring evening, he had never encountered a spirit.

After seeing the lady by the sea Gregson said,

"There is no doubt about them now. I am certain of what I saw. I returned to the place the next day and checked out all the rock formations to make sure I was not mistaken."

Anthony Gregson made another decision. He vowed not to return to the spot.

"I believe in leaving ghosts to their own lives. I am not going back there again. It was an unnerving experience."

The episode at Oak Bay has all the ingredients of a classic ghost story. The basic characteristics in this single incident are supported by reports from all over the world. There is a distinct pattern to such appearances. A sudden, unexplained mood change preceded the actual manifestation of the spirit. The humans involved feel or sense the presence of something unnatural before they actually see it. The ghost is able to move with incredible speed and grace. Its movement is without any apparent physical effort or strain. The spirit is not even required to touch the ground as it moves. Frequently there is no sound to the spectral passage — the action is silent and smooth.

Following the sighting, most people involved begin to doubt the evidence of their own senses, just as Anthony Gregson did. They seek the support and reassurance of anyone who is with them. Then the decision is often made to try to forget the entire incident. A thing which challenges the credulity to such an extent should be ignored, they feel.

In this case, one is left wondering if Gregson and his friend might have witnessed a reenactment of the 1936 tragedy if they had stayed longer.

A later story, written by Diane Janowski in the Daily Colonist, reported that the tragic phantom was seen by at least seven people in May, 1968.

A few more details of the unfortunate woman's death are provided in this account. The husband had a drinking problem and the wife planned to divorce him. Some time after this announcement she was found strangled and beaten and lying in the bushes near the eighth tee of Victoria Golf Course. The husband was found in the same area, drowned.

Almost every year, apparently, somebody sights the gray and misty lady and the controversy breaks out all over again.

According to the 1968 report, sixteen-year-old Ann Smith was walking on the golf course with some friends when the spirit appeared. Ann screamed. She described the ghost as short, noiseless and chilly.

The same group of friends visited the spot the following night and the phantom obligingly reappeared. This time, Ann walked toward her. The ghost vanished. A sailor who was with the group stated that he knew what swamp gas looked like and this was definitely not swamp gas. While these witnesses were sure they saw a ghost, others were equally sure it was only fog or spring blossoms. In Oak Bay, every spring, you can decide either way.

SPIRIT OF SUMMERLAND

One of the clues about a ghost as opposed to a real human is that it makes no noise when it walks. This silent, smooth movement is repeated in many stories in every part of the world.

It was the silent progress of a lonely male walker that made two British Columbia boys think he wasn't real at all, but that they had seen a spirit passing by.

During the First World War, the Richards family (not their real name) lived on a farm near Summerland, British Columbia. The farm was a lonely location, being on a secondary road that came to a dead end just beyond the limits of their property.

The Richards' land was a gently rolling apple orchard. Adjacent to the orchard lay five acres of unused land fed by an irrigating flume which caused the grass there to be particularly lush. It was a logical place to tether the family saddle horse.

The tethering of the horse had to be changed regularly

and this was a chore which the two Richards boys did together at the end of each day.

One moonlight summer night around eleven o'clock, Sam, 14 and Edward, 20 walked to the pastureland to move their horse. They moved the animal to a spot about one hundred feet from the winding road leading back towards their house.

Sam Richards still remembers that night vividly.

"While my brother attended to the tethering of the horse, I was wandering about with nothing to do. I looked down the road. I saw a man coming up the road toward me. He was dressed in white. I was surprised that we'd be having a strange visitor so late. When he came directly opposite to me I called out, 'Where are you going?' He stopped, turned and faced me. Then he walked towards our house without speaking. I wasn't disturbed because he didn't answer me, it was the fact that he made no sound when he walked away from us."

Mr. Richards described the stranger as fairly heavy-set, wearing a white coat in the style of a Norfolk jacket.

"I watched him go toward our house but because the door was on the other side of the house we couldn't see where he went. After Edward tethered the horse, we hurried up to the house. We asked our folks if anyone had called. They hadn't seen anyone, nor had they heard a knock at the main door. Whatever-it-was had simply vanished behind the building."

Mr. Richards' description of his unexpected visitor makes him sound like a rather elegant country gentleman from the 1890-1900 period. The silent approach, the fact that he didn't speak or change his course indicates that the spirit may have been familiar with the road. Perhaps he walked that path many times in the past. The Richards farm may have been on the site of some old residence in the area and the two boys may just have happened to be there when the man took his favorite evening stroll.

Chapter Three

DEMON DOGS AND GIGGLING GIRLS

ANY TIME, ANY PLACE

What is a ghost? The meaning of the word depends largely upon the area in which the sighting or occurrence takes place. It can also be influenced by the background, religious upbringing and national origin of the persons directly involved in the actual manifestation. Generally, the term is used to refer to the ethereal presentation, seen or sensed, of a dead person to the living — or to what we might call an apparition.

On a broader plane, the term "ghost" has been used to refer to all psychic manifestations and their related phenomena. In this latter category, one finds incidents of telepathy, clairvoyance, precognition, hindsight, astral wanderings and the different versions of the unpopular poltergeist. All of these phenomena have occurred in Canada within the past ten years.

The primary characteristics accorded to ghosts are internationally consistent to quite a large extent. The Chinese, for example, firmly believe that all creatures have spirits, so it is not too surprising to discover that their ghosts often appear in animal form or shape. Our Canadian folklore tends to support this theory; we have claimed to have our own Demon Dog, ghostly horses, cats and dogs and even the occasional bird. Stories about a mighty spirit-wolf are told by the French Canadians. But, for the most part, our ghosts tend to assume human form when they materialize.

The ghosts of the Chinese are often indistinguishable from living persons. Once again, our findings lead us to concur with their beliefs. People have been known to walk right past apparitions without being aware of the startling significance of their experience until a later time.

Contrary to popular belief, ghostly appearances are not restricted to the hours of darkness. They may occur anywhere, at any time — day or night — and are highly unpredictable. Experiences may occur singly, in series or widely separated in time and they are frequently accompanied by other disturbing and unusual sensations.

No haunting is ever totally like any other. Since ghosts differ from each other as much as living persons, the characteristics which precede their individual manifestation also vary to a marked degree.

A ghost can become known by the secondary traits that accompany each consecutive appearance. Observers have reported odd smells, ranging from sickly sweet to subtly floral. Some spirits even smell of tobacco smoke or burning leaves. Frequently visual, audible and tactile experiences are all involved in a single sighting. A ghost is like a very talented musician — it can play with striking effect upon all of the human senses.

A ghostly assault upon the ears can be most impressive. All manner of sounds echo from the past up into the present. Digging, fighting, screaming, banging and invisible musical renditions are among those most commonly heard.

The sound of footsteps is another favourite. Trying to follow ghostly footsteps can be an unnerving experience. This is especially true if they seem to move from one part of the house to another as soon as the first place has been thoroughly checked out. The investigator knows that, somehow, the invisible noisemaker has passed right by him, or through him, in the connecting corridors. A relatively common occurrence in hauntings, this is the sort of incident which can utterly devastate people who are used to believing only that which they can actually see or touch.

Apparitions involving children are frequently preceded by the sounds of running footsteps and childish laughter or giggling. This is particularly true if the house has been a happy place in the past.

Many buildings have been known to assume an atmosphere consistent with their history. Hence, some dwellings just seem welcoming and comfortable as soon as you enter them. Others are downright frightening. For not all small figures from the spirit world bring joy and merriment with them. The sound of crying can be heard late at night, and concerned listeners may even experience a strange feeling of deep sadness and depression if their house is occupied by an unhappy little spirit.

The number of sightings of ghost children has greatly decreased over the years. This is only natural. Social pressures, increased education and improved medical techniques and facilities have cut down on the incidents involving them in sudden or extremely painful death. Still, we have received reports of children appearing from the past. Many died long ago; others seem to have died more recent'y. Clothing and hair style help in some cases, but often there is no way of accurately determining their origin.

Some child spirits are accompanied by the ghosts of older persons who may have died at the same time. It is possible, but as yet unproven, that some of these mature spirits are relatives from even farther back in history.

Occasionally people have trouble with an empty cradle. It will suddenly begin to rock as if it were actually occupied by a baby at that very moment. Attempts to stop the rocking motion are met with definite resistance. The action continues unabated.

There are many women wandering about on the astral plane. In fact, it sometimes seems as though there are more female ghosts than male ones. Any number of reasons can be offered for this apparent oddity —but none of them has yet been proven. It is possible that the female ghosts are simply more active and sociable than their male counterparts.

HITCHHIKING SPIRITS

Some of the ghostly women merely appear along the side of the road at dusk. Others, bolder, have been known to hitchhike to a place where they once lived. They then vanish somewhere between the conveyance and the front door of the residence. Unless the driver has a reason for making inquiries within the house, he may never even know that he has driven a ghost home that evening.

A sense of duty seems to motivate many of the female ghosts. Some women come back to care for small children that they have had to leave behind. This is most common when the children are being poorly raised or mistreated by a stranger.

The feminine urge to meddle does not cease with death. In a very few reported cases, men have remarried, only to be caused great embarrassment and personal distress by the hauntings of their first wives.

Most of the ghostly women are unaccompanied, but this is not always the case. Some carry babies that died with them, and others appear with husbands or lovers who shared their deaths.

A persistent belief in our Canadian folklore is that a patch of strange, glowing light may be a prelude to the visual manifestation of a spirit. These illuminated sightings have been blamed upon the presence of marsh gases in the area. And this reasoning does have some basis in fact. Sudden flickers of light can spring from methane, and this substance forms the main composite of marsh gases.

In still other instances, unnatural light attributed to the forces of the supernatural may have been caused by luminous phosphorus issuing from old and rotting tree stumps.

Marsh gases and tree stumps are both perfectly logical explanations. And they could well account for a certain percentage of the strange stories we have heard. What leads us back to the possibility of supernatural illumination, however, is the fact that sightings have been recorded and investigated in areas where no such stumps or gases exist.

Marsh gases have been used in recent attempts to explain unidentified flying objects in some of the western provinces. Once again, the explanation is reasonable but not applicable in all cases. Unusual atmospheric conditions explain away many incidents, but enough remain unsolved to make one consider that the forces of the supernatural might have been involved.

Ghosts are cold. Those encountering psychic phenomena notice sudden, unexplainable chills or pervading drafts during the course of a manifestation. It is almost as if someone had left a door open in midwinter and the entire area had grown icy as a result. This is one of the more common characteristics of apparitions. The resultant cold does not seem natural, and can be most uncomfortable.

It may be that the spirit gains additional energy by draining and utilizing the warmth from its surroundings. And, since sudden temperature changes can be fatal to tropical fish, it is not too surprising to hear of the deaths of goldfish and their ilk after the appearance of a spectre in their immediate vicinity.

The same unnatural chill may also be the origin of such catch-phrases as "goose-bumps", and "the hair stood up on the back of my neck." The individual is simply reacting physically to the abnormal temperature in his environment. Now that we are searching for new energy sources, it might be very helpful if we could just figure out how a spirit utilizes air temperature at will.

Attempts to shoot, injure, or otherwise deter a ghost can prove both frustrating and ineffective. How can you possibly apply a physical handicap to something that is already dead and disembodied? To shoot at a spectre is not only useless; it can be dangerous under certain circumstances. The bullet could ricochet off a wall to hit the person holding the weapon.

Some people believe that it is helpful to ask a wandering spirit to reveal its purpose "in the name of God", others think that you should simply ignore the apparition and hope that it will go away.

On occasion, psychics and mediums use a series of word pictures which seem to release earthbound spirits. The emphasis is placed on the soothing ideas associated with the color green. They suggest that the troubled spirit imagine green leaves, green grass and green trees. Then they direct the ghost to follow the light above the trees to freedom and "home".

There are no hard and fast rules for ridding oneself and one's residence of an unwanted spirit. Sufficient attempts have been made at exorcism to indicate that this may only be effective if the ghost has completed its task and was a religious person during its lifetime. That information may be hard to obtain. Even then, there is no guarantee of success for this sort of operation. It is like being rude to a guest in the hope that he will realize he is not wanted and leave. The guest may take offense at your bad manners and decide to stay for sheer spite. The exorcism rite, expelling a spirit by means of invocation, may only anger the ghost and increase the degree of abnormal activity. Its effects cannot be predicted with any accuracy and can be quite devastating.

WHO WILL COME BACK?

There does not seem to be any particular formula for determining who can or will return from the dead. For all we know, these apparitions may be merely in a state of transition prior to their reincarnation. If this is indeed the case, an indeterminate number of variables must be involved, for the period of transition or ghosthood can vary markedly. Sometimes it lasts only a short period and involves a single appearance, or it can encompass a great many years and numerous sightings.

Certainly we would be in an impossible situation if all those who had died tragically, or in great physical or mental agony, were to suddenly reappear in our midst. Some areas would be totally overrun by ghosts, a veritable infestation of lost spirits, because of a single large and violent historical event. All former battlefields, instead of just a few, would be untenable for living humans. Nor would houses be exempt in the case of a massive ghostly takeover. Almost every family would have at least one spectre left over from somewhere in the past.

Fortunately, however, this does not seem to be what happens. Many individuals have died unpleasantly, in both peace and war, and the vast majority of them have never been recorded as ghosts. Nor are all wrongdoers haunted and persecuted while they remain near the scene of their former criminal acts.

Henry the Eighth would have had a frightful time if this had been the standard procedure. As far as we can determine, none of his victims ever returned to demand personal vengeance. Anne Boleyn has been reported to pace the ramparts of the Tower, startling present-day guards, but she apparently did not trouble Henry during his remaining years.

There are exceptions to every rule, however. Wicked lives may end — not in the supposed peace of the grave, but in the vicious circle of a never-ending penance exacted for past sins. Labrador has such a spirit. He is a ghostly trapper who pays eternally for his evil earthly existence. He was the direct cause of much heartbreak, injury and death during his lifetime. Not only was he guilty of supplying bad, and often fatal, alcohol throughout the northern territories, he also attacked local women when their men were away tending to trap lines in the bush country. This man was every inch a storybook villain with no good qualities ever being discovered to offset the bad ones.

FOURTEEN WHITE HUSKIES

The trapper died a natural death but he has been seen by many people. Every story contains the same information. He is observed driving a matched team of fourteen pure white huskies through the snow. This detail is consistent with his past history and character as he did once take great pride in his dogs; a collection of white huskies.

All those who see the trapper have been helped by him. His apparent task is to seek, find and guide lost travellers and trappers through the mighty blizzards until they reach a place of safety. This accomplished, he then disappears into the raging storm from which he came.

Credited with saving many lives, the mysterious trapper was last reported making his ghostly rounds in 1959. On that occasion, he helped a young man reach the safety of a hunting lodge. When the man turned at the door to thank his rescuer, the trapper had vanished.

Ghosts make requests for special and sometimes unorthodox burial procedures. In March of 1972, a group of five people living in a small northern Manitoba town had trouble. They complained that they were being haunted by the ghost of a dead relative. They claimed loudly that the woman, in the form of an apparition, appeared every night. She said that she was unable to rest. The reason for her restlessness was that they had buried her in the same grave with her estranged husband who had predeceased her by six years. Even death had failed to end the lifetime quarrel between husband and wife.

Local civil and clerical authorities were consulted, and much discussion and argument ensued. Eventually the problem was solved. Permission was granted to meet the demands of the unhappy spirit. The woman's remains were exhumed and placed in another grave. And, since that time, the relatives claim that they have been allowed to sleep peacefully and unmolested.

It is not usually this simple to translate the wishes of a spirit into action.

Other apparitions may return just to create a bit of confusion, casually occupying a favourite rocking chair or fireside corner. These visitors seem to relish listening to relatives discuss their past existence, and can react violently to unfavorable references. Other spirits want only to be allowed to remain, quietly and inoffensively, for a period of time which can vary radically according to the whims of each individual spectre.

WICKEDNESS REVEALED

Many of the reported cases of ghostly vengeance have been attributed to the guilty consciences and vivid imaginations of those involved in the original offence. And it is almost certain that those who believe in curses, hexes and angry ghosts are more likely to be struck down by them. The mind which truly believes itself to be guilty and deserving of punishment can exact a fearful price from the individual. Occasionally a sense of guilt or shame has resulted in a total loss of sanity. But this does not account for the numerous sightings in which quite innocent and uninvolved persons have been led by spectral figures to the hitherto undiscovered scene of some ghastly crime against humanity.

Generally apparitions appear in places where they were happiest, or most miserable, or at the scene of some major occurrence in which they were directly and seriously involved. They have revealed accurate information too many times in too many different places to be dismissed as mere hallucination or imagination. In many cases the actions seem deliberate.

It might be wise to consider this particular aspect of the supernatural and the other possible consequences before committing an offensive or wicked act. There is no guarantee that killing a person will stop him from all future activity. Many wrongdoers have experienced horrifying ordeals which indicate that the dead can, and sometimes do, return to provide unorthodox but highly convincing testimony against those who persecuted them in life.

PACTS

The general format of death pacts is usually the same in each case. The first person to die agrees to attempt to communicate by any means available with those who have been left behind. And those remaining are to be available, alert and receptive to the message.

Perhaps we ought to pay more attention to people who vow to return from the grave. For it would appear that this sort of mutual arrangement can actually be effected. Such appearances are usually of brief duration. They seldom develop into a full-scale, lasting problem with haunting. Once the required message is passed on, acknowledged and understood, the faithful spirit seems content to leave of its own volition.

A classic example of pact fulfillment took place in Nova Scotia during the nineteen forties. It involved two women, Rita and Agnes, who had gone through public school together, through high school and who had worked together in the same large business office in Halifax.

Being of a somewhat imaginative and romantic nature, they vowed that if one should die first, she would return and make herself known to her friend. This, they agreed, would prove conclusively that ghosts did exist.

Both girls married, and Rita remained in Halifax while Agnes moved to Sydney. When she was only thirty-two, Agnes died. The year was 1947.

On a particularly warm June night, Rita found herself alone in her two-storey house in a suburb of Halifax. It was a charming house and one of the nicest architectural features was a pleasant little alcove beside the staircase. The alcove was in deep shadows, and yet there was still a faint wash of fading daylight. Rita was about to climb the stairs when she saw a shape in the alcove.

Her first reaction was fear. A prowler, perhaps, had broken into the house. But the shape took a clearer form and she saw her childhood friend, Agnes, looking young and serene. Agnes smiled.

Rita tried to speak to her friend but before she could utter a word, Agnes vanished. Still, it was enough to convince Rita that her friend had returned from the grave to keep the pact they had made so many years ago.

Chapter Four

ONTARIO GHOSTS

DEATH OF TOM THOMSON

Not all ghosts are frightening.

There have been several cases in which violent or unusual deaths have led to non-violent hauntings in the years that followed the actual incident. One such case tells of a man who, having died tragically and suddenly, returns without apparent malice to the area where he spent many of the happiest and most creative years of his short life.

The ghost of Tom Thomson, the landscape artist, has been seen on quiet evenings at dusk. He wears a favourite shirt, easily recognizable from old snapshots of that period, and silently paddles his grey canoe near the scene of his most mysterious death.

The actual circumstances surrounding Thomson's death on July 8, 1917, have never been discovered. Nor is it likely that they ever will be as most of the possible witnesses have since died.

An expert canoeist, Thomson was found "drowned" under most unusual circumstances. There was no water in his lungs. Some fishing line was wrapped sixteen or seventeen times around his left ankle. This in itself was odd. And, since the man was very much aware of the rules regarding safe swimming, fishing and boating, it has been doubted that he ever tied the amateurish knots that held his portage paddle in place. He simply knew better. Nor could Tom's friends account for a large bump on his head.

Up until the time he died, Thomson had been staying at Mowat Lodge. It was an old frame building, since burned down, on the west shore of Canoe Lake. That day, Tom had told Mark Robinson, Chief Park Ranger, that he was going trout fishing on nearby Gill Lake. As far as we know, he never reached Gill Lake.

Two Park guides, George Rowe and Lowrie Dixon, found Thomson's body eight days after the artist had disappeared. The body was buried rather hurriedly in Algonquin Park by the residents who had befriended Tom and watched his talent develop over the years.

After the burial, an inquest was held in one of the cottages. The local coroner never viewed the body and the ensuing events were equally peculiar.

One of those who testified at the inquest was a German-American. Residents told of a recent and violent quarrel between this man and Thomson. They thought that the subject of the quarrel might have been either the First World War, then being fought, or Tom's girl friend, Winifred Trainor.

The evening following Tom's burial, a lone man appeared in the Park. He had an order to have the artist's remains shipped elsewhere. This stranger to the area worked unassisted for several hours by the lonely graveside. He was driven by the proprietor of Mowat Lodge back to the railway station early the next morning. Shannon Fraser supplied his wagon and his own services as driver. He insisted later that the coffin-box which he helped load onto the train was not heavy enough to have contained a body. There had not been sufficient time or manpower to have completed the job so quickly. Local residents were of the opinion that Thomson's body was never moved. Where his remains were finally laid to rest is still a mystery.

A disinterment of the body supposedly buried at Leath, Ontario, might help. It might determine if Tom's remains were ever transferred from the Park; it would not solve the mystery of his recurring ghost. Many claim that the spirit of Thomson lingers on in the Park, in the forest country he loved so well and where he died before his time.

Although Thomson died a violent and most unexpected death, he does not appear to be seeking vengeance. Nor does he seem to wish any harm to come upon those who inadvertently encounter him in the Park. He simply disappears, leaving them to doubt their senses. Fortunately for us, more than one person has seen this particular apparition during the course of a single appearance. Reluctantly and with some embarrassment, they have corroborated each other's stories.

On one occasion, the lone grey canoe was seen landing on a beach near Hayhurst Point. Those trying to follow it brought their canoes right in behind. But they could find no markings at all near that spot. The canoe was gone!

Oddly enough, Thomson's real canoe, also grey, vanished shortly after his death. A thorough search of the area by campers, guides and rangers produced many canoes of different shapes, colours and sizes. Thomson's canoe was not among them.

The scene now is a peaceful one, well-loved by painters and zealously defended by naturalists and environmentalists. A boat tour carries sightseers past the places where Thomson worked on his paintings. Miss Algonquin, a glass-domed excursion boat, is operated by Boat Tours International of Toronto. It departs from the Canoe Lake Portage Store and crosses the lake to cruise past two memorials erected for Thomson on Hayhurst Point. It goes past the old dock from which the artist departed on his final fishing trip. The boat visits the cabins of Mark Robinson and Tom's girl friend and, after passing the spot where his body was discovered, returns to the docks of the Portage Store.

BEATRICE, A DETERMINED SPIRIT

Can a very determined lady who is officially dead, return to her childhood home and take over its management? In the case of Beatrice Simms, a religious spinster who died in 1967, it seems entirely possible.

The three-storey house on Colborne Street in London, Ontario, began to change not long after Beatrice's death. Beatrice had loved the house; she wanted to live there for the remainder of her life. In 1943, however, she was forced to sell it because of financial problems. Her parents had died and her brother had left home. Beatrice had to admit that she could no longer maintain the large house by herself.

The ownership of the house changed several times during Beatrice's lifetime. None of the owners noticed anything the least bit psychic or unusual about the building; it was just another large and comfortable house to them. But when Beatrice died, the trouble began.

Beatrice died in Toronto, but she had vowed to her friends that she would return to the London house.

Late in the summer of 1967, the Richard Saunders family occupied the Simms house. (The name of the family has been changed but all other names and times are factual).

The Saunders were a sensible and practical couple. At that time, they knew nothing whatever about ghosts; nor were they much interested in the subject. You would not have found their names on the membership lists of any spiritualist organizations. They had never heard of Beatrice Simms and had no complaints about the house itself or the neighborhood.

During September, that same year, the Saunders began to hear and sense strange things. Doors creaked for no reason and the sound of light footsteps echoed throughout the house.

At first, Mr. Saunders was skeptical. He thought that his wife was only suffering from nervous exhaustion ; she was a woman with a new baby and two other small children. His attitude underwent an abrupt change one day when he was alone in the house. He could clearly hear someone calling his name. The house was empty, and there was no one in the yard.

From that day on, the sounds and sensations gradually increased. Disembodied voices would call out unexpectedly from some unoccupied room in the old house.

Mr. and Mrs. Saunders were sure that they felt another presence right there in the house with them. Without being aware of exactly what was going on, they were still positive that something unnatural was happening in their home. The mood of the house was actually changing. And these alterations were being made by someone or something that the Saunders could not even see.

The three Saunders children were all babies. Under four years of age, it was obvious to everyone that they were far too young to be held responsible for the strange occurrences.

The family dog, a German Shepherd named Chimo, began to act in a most peculiar way. He would stand motionless, a picture of frozen terror, at the head of the main stairs. A well-behaved, friendly and dependable animal for years, Chimo now refused to respond when the Saunders called him. He would just stand there staring out into empty space.

On Hallowe'en night, the dog vanished completely. No trace of him was ever found. While it is possible that Chimo might have been involved in a traffic accident, dogs in London are required to carry a license. Surely the Saunders would have received some sort of notification. It seems more likely that the poor animal simply could not endure the dreadful atmosphere any longer. He was quite literally scared away. Could he perhaps have seen something that was invisible to the Saunders?

Next the budgie and two goldfish died for no apparent reason. Mr. and Mrs. Saunders were becoming thoroughly concerned about the safety of their small children. Something or somebody was obviously infiltrating their home and upsetting the entire family. It seemed too much of a coincidence to lose all their household pets within such a short period. They had no idea what would happen next, and lived in a constant state of suspense and fear.

The footsteps continued. An increasingly frequent occurrence, they usually sounded as if some person were slowly and deliberately ascending the central staircase. The sounds would cease just before the invisible climber would normally have crossed into a watcher's line of vision.

During that memorable winter, a visitor to the Saunders' house listened in disbelief to these strange footsteps as she stood at the head of the stairs. There was no one there at all. She could see the entire stairway stretched out below her, and could hear the footsteps growing louder as they approached her. But she saw nothing to account for the footsteps, and hid with the little children under the nearest bed.

Voices continued to call out at night and even during the daytime. Sometimes they sounded like those of adults but occasionally they were quite childlike. Neighbors recall being clearly told, "Come right on in," when Mrs. Saunders, occupied elsewhere in the large house, was equally positive that she had not even heard them knock at the front door. At times such as this, it seemed as though someone other than herself had assumed complete control of the household. And that was a most disconcerting idea.

On New Year's Eve, Richard Saunders and his wife decided to go out. They wanted to get away from the house in order to greet 1968 in a proper frame of mind. By that time, Mrs. Saunders was very much in need of an evening away from the endless confusion that now marked her days at home.

The Saunders' regular daytime baby-sitter and another local girl reluctantly agreed to stay with the children that evening. Perhaps they hoped that there might be some security in numbers.

When Mr. and Mrs. Saunders left, they carefully locked the front door after themselves. The wary teenagers checked the door from the inside just to reassure themselves that everything was securely locked.

One of the girls went upstairs to check on the children. Her friend remained in the livingroom. They both heard the front door open and close, although they knew that such a thing was quite impossible. Knowing how frightened the girls were, the Saunders would have rung the doorbell if they had forgotten something and had to return. No one else was supposed to have a key.

The baby-sitters stayed where they were, one upstairs and one down. They listened intently. Someone walked slowly and firmly across the entrance hall and then entered the little backshed used for storage.

A ROCKING CHAIR

Then the young girls were astonished to hear the sound of a rocking chair in motion. But that back door to the shed was still so securely latched that the combined weight of the two baby-sitters could not have forced it open. Nor was there any way for them to have known that Mrs. Saunders had placed an old rocking chair out there just the day before.

But, if no one could open the door and no one knew about the rocking chair, who or what was responsible for the noises in the little shed ?

After that unnerving experience, the baby-sitters absolutely refused to return. They had no desire to chance further incidents.

Mrs. Saunders began to get increasingly frightened and nervous. Several times, she felt a strong compulsion to simply run outside with the children. And she would suddenly feel a very cold sensation right against her back or following her about as she worked in the kitchen.

No logical explanations could be found to explain all the strange happenings. Whatever had invaded the Saunders home seemed determined to force them to move away. And there was a fair chance, at this stage, that the intruder might be successful.

It was at this highly critical point that Mr. and Mrs. Saunders were finally told about the late Beatrice Simms. They learned of her intense, overriding, desire to return home. After some searching, the Saunders found books and papers bearing Beatrice's name, in a remote corner of the attic. They considered the matter carefully and concluded that the old rocker in the shed might once have belonged to Beatrice.

"After that, I sort of took a friendly attitude towards this whatever-it-was in our house," said Mrs. Saunders.

She began to talk calmly to the ghost whenever she felt its presence near her.

"You could feel something watching. You just knew something was standing there by the railing at the top of the stairs."

A number of times, she asked if the visitor might be the spirit or ghost of Beatrice Simms. There was no noticeable response to the question.

As far as she can recall, Mrs. Saunders never actually went so far as to officially order the ghost to leave her home. She does admit that she might have suggested this on one of the many occasions when the thing got on her nerves. The spirit might have taken offence "once when I got real mad and may have told it to get out!"

No one conducted a seance to try to make meaningful contact with the spirit of Beatrice. The Saunders still knew nothing about such things. There was not even any mention of trying to exorcise the spirit.

The Saunders did not learn about exorcism and its reputed effectiveness until some time later. By then, their personal period of supernatural crisis was over, and they had no need for the information.

Whatever the reason, things began to settle back to normal in February of 1968.

"The house felt different, and we could sense it wasn't there anymore. But I was nearly a nervous wreck!" said Mrs. Saunders.

So maybe Beatrice did get her own way in the end. Perhaps she did manage to return after all those years of hoping and planning, only to find herself highly unwelcome and her old room occupied by a new baby. How

disappointed she must have been! She still possessed
enormous staying power to remain so long in the old
house. The various voices, footsteps and creaking doors
did not take place on only several occasions. They occurred with some regularity, several times each week for five
months.

The Saunders seem unchanged by their experience;
they still look for natural explanations for what happened.
In discussing the various incidents with reporters, they
do not say that they believe in ghosts. Nor do they claim,
as one might expect, that their house was actually haunted
for a definite period of time. They will only say that all
of these highly unusual things really did happen, and that
the events did coincide with the aftermath of Beatrice
Simm's death in Toronto.

Failing to frighten off these strangers in her old home,
the spirit of this very determined woman must have finally
decided not to stay where she was unwelcome. Her
disappearance from the house pleased the Saunders, but
she did leave behind some minor mysteries for interested
people to ponder.

Of course, we do not know for sure that the spirit in
the Saunders house was that of Beatrice. Given the story
of Beatrice's determination, however, and the coincidence
of her death and the beginning of the disturbance in the
London house, we can only make a reasonable guess. It
would seem that Beatrice came home, thereby fulfilling
her previously made vow.

BLOODSTAINS ON THE KITCHEN FLOOR

In late May of 1963, strange things began to happen
for no apparent reason in the Keswick, Ontario home
of the Frederick Matthews family.

The Matthews home is an old frame building. It has
seen more than fifty years of life pass through its many
halls. Mrs. Matthews, who is not a superstitious woman
under ordinary circumstances, was totally at a loss when
asked to explain the odd events. She tried in vain to find

a connection between the incidents and a streak of bad luck in the family.

"We have had a lot of bad luck since we moved into this house thirteen years ago. But lately our luck has been changing. Perhaps all these unusual happenings are an evil spirit preparing to leave the house."

A dark stain, forming a skull and cross-bones design, appeared on the kitchen floor. No one had spilled anything; nor could they think of a natural explanation to account for the mark. To further complicate things, another stain appeared on one of the kitchen chairs. Seemingly caused by the same substance, this stain looked quite a bit like a woman wearing an old-fashioned hoop skirt.

Dishes rattled about night and day. Cupboard doors began to open and close without warning or human touch. The sound of unexplained knocking was frequently heard at the front door.

No natural explanations could be found for the weird vibrations and knockings.

A neighbor suggested that Mrs. Matthews use a Bible to quell the disturbance. It didn't work. The presence of an open Bible only intensified the noises and actually seemed to make the stains grow brighter. On the more practical side, prolonged and powerful scrubbing of the problem areas failed to reduce the size or coloration of the stubborn stains. Perversely, just when everyone was about to give up the effort, the stains would simply disappear and later reappear of their own accord.

The deliberate nature of such incidents led the people involved to the belief that there had to be some sort of intelligence behind the occurrences. It was an agent that seemed to understand just when a sudden reversal of tactics would be most effective and unnerving. Whatever was in the house seemed capable of thought.

After her disappointing, but not too surprising, failure with the Bible, Mrs. Matthews thought the matter over very carefully. She decided to do absolutely nothing about her resident spirit. She was hoping that it would simply go away by itself, without any further effort on her part. A wise woman, Mrs. Matthews did not wish to risk antagonizing something about which she had no understanding or knowledge.

Mrs. Matthews must have accidentally hit upon the right idea when she decided not to interfere with the activities of her ghost. The sound effects diminished as the dishes gradually ceased their banging. The stubborn stains began to fade and then totally disappeared. Even the knocking at the front door stopped.

There were no further reports of difficulty from the Matthews' home.

Nothing is known about the Keswick house that could possibly account for this haunting or for the unusual symbols and designs made by the recurrent stains. Of course, the interpretation of shapes made by blotches or stains is an uncertain business at best; two people might have entirely different ideas as to the meaning of a single shape. So, while the stains were certainly an indication that something was wrong in the house, I think we can safely discount any significance people might attribute to their specific shapes. Besides, Keswick was never pirate country.

There is no known record of violent death having occurred on the Keswick premises, despite indications of one in the kitchen. This incident remains a mystery. Mrs. Matthews' theory about an evil spirit preparing for departure is unusual, but it is as good an explanation as any other. If this was a poltergeist, it was a mild one. But, as Mrs. Matthews pointed out, the strange events were preceded by thirteen years of bad luck.

A BROWN AND EGG-SHAPED THING

Does a ghost always have to represent a dead person ? Is it possible that a human being who is still alive can project some part of the spirit to another location and cause a haunting?

There is no way of knowing for sure, but that idea has been advanced as the explanation for a series of terrifying and unusual incidents in Etobicoke, a suburb of Toronto.

In May, 1968, two families occupied a large, 80-year-old farmhouse on Prince Edward Drive. The names of these people have been changed because they were so harassed by curious mobs when the story was first published in the Toronto newspapers, that it seems kindest to protect them, even now.

Edward Craighill and his wife rented the house for $250 a month. Living with them was their ten-year-old daughter, Anne. The second floor apartment was sub-let to their 27-year-old daughter, Diana and her husband, John Bullen. The Bullens had two small daughters. The Craighills also rented out the basement to a bachelor schoolteacher. These financial arrangements suited everybody. The Craighills liked the house, too, and had no intention of moving.

Despite the pleasant situation, life took an ugly turn one warm May night. Diana Bullen, in one of the second-floor bedrooms, woke up in the night to hear heavy footsteps in the attic.

"I heard the footsteps, thump, thump, thump. Next I heard screeching laughter. It sounded like a middle-aged woman was right in the room with me."

She awakened John. They both listened to the sounds, terrified. Then they got to up check on the two little girls asleep in the other bedroom. The noise stopped. The little girls had not heard anything and neither had the Craighills asleep on the main floor. Early the next morning the family searched the attic and found nothing. Diana Bullen eventually went back to bed to try to get some of the sleep she'd missed during the night.

While still half-asleep, Mrs. Bullen suddenly felt that someone was standing over her. There was nobody to be seen. She felt a sudden chill.

"I felt as if somebody had walked right through me." She said.

The next night the thumping began again. This time it was two in the morning. It was a slow, confident step and it continued until dawn.

The Bullens decided to visit friends the following night and so they did not sleep in the house, but they came back the next day. That night was the worst yet.

It began at twelve-thirty. First the footsteps and then the screeching. Finally, John Bullen spoke, telling whatever it was to keep quiet. The noise stopped and the Bullens went back to sleep. But at four a.m. they awoke again. This time the cat, Fluffy, walked out of the bedroom toward the attic door. The closed door was just out of the line of vision from the bedroom. The Bullens heard a thump as if the cat had been kicked and then the cat screamed as if in terror or pain. This was followed by screaming which sounded human, and then by horrible laughter.

John Bullen got out of bed.

"Is the cat dead?" Diana asked him.

John found the cat stunned and leaning against the wall. Its long fur was standing straight out as if the cat had been given an electrical shock. The animal was staring at the door leading to the attic.

The Bullens did go back to bed but they did not sleep well. John called his wife during the day from the factory where he worked. Diana told him that, unfortunately, everything was not alright. She heard the footsteps during the day and now there was light outside the closed attic door. She was so upset she went out to tell a neighbor, Ron Leyzack. He got his .22 calibre rifle and invaded the attic but found nothing.

It was apparently one of the neighbors, now aware of the problem in the Craighill house, who telephoned a Toronto newspaper. Since ghosts are always good copy, two reporters, both experienced men, were despatched to cover the story. John Downing and John Gault, representing the Toronto Telegram, and filled with the usual skepticism of the press, arrived late in the afternoon to check out the attic and interview the two families living in the house.

In the attic they found nothing. It was a square room with a sloping roof and with no openings which would allow an animal to get in. The footsteps and the noises could not be explained. They decided to stay the night in the house.

As a precaution against fraud, the two reporters covered the attic floor with flour. The idea was that if human feet were making those thumping noises, the flour would be disturbed. At three-thirty in the morning they heard the walking. The cat was crying. They checked the flour-covered floor and found no foot prints.

The following day The Reverend Tom Bartlett of the Star of Progress Spiritualist Church was invited to the house to investigate the mystery. He arrived with his wife, Pat, and both were fascinated with the challenge.

Mr. Bartlett climbed up into the attic alone. It was, by this time, dusk and the attic was gloomy. The door to the attic was closed on him. He stood for a few minutes in silence and then, glancing slightly to his left, he saw a brown, egg-shaped form. It was luminous, providing its own light.

The form he later described as about four feet by two feet. It moved slowly from his left side to his right. Then it hovered beside him. He called for his wife to join him in the attic.

When Pat Bartlett's eyes adjusted to the darkness she, too, saw the form. It was on her left but she saw it as a brownish yard-stick, about two or three inches wide. At the same time, Mrs. Bartlett felt a sharp pain in her stomach and chest. A thump was heard at this time.

(Down below, at the closed attic door, there was also activity. Diana Bullen, standing with the two reporters, saw a light at the door. The reporters confirmed that they, too, saw the light. Everybody felt intensely cold).

The two reporters joined the Bartletts in the attic

but somebody put on lights, and it was then impossible to see the brown, mysterious form. The Bartletts described what they had seen, and said that they thought the shape was trying to direct their attention to a dormer window which overlooked the back yard.

Mr. Bartlett theorized that the egg-shaped thing might be a thought form, and both Bartletts considered the possibility that the color brown signified that the spirit was still attached to the earth but that it was sick.

The Bartletts performed an exorcism service and then everybody prepared to leave the house. At this point, though, Diana Bullen became hysterical and fainted. She was, according to the reporters, in a semi-faint for at least half an hour. And by four o'clock in the morning the footsteps were heard once more. Mrs. Craighill then saw a light at the top of the stairs which led to the second-floor apartment. She said,

"We are all petrified now."

The following day the Craighills telephoned their landlord and reluctantly told him they were giving notice. When they told him the reason, the landlord's son volunteered to stay in the house overnight to find out for himself what all the fuss was about.

The reporters, the landlord's son, and the two families stayed once more in the house. Downing and Gault, the two newsmen, rigged up a network of invisible threads in the attic and attached bells to the ends. They reasoned that if a real, strong draft blew through the attic, the bells would ring. If a human was causing the disturbance he would have difficulty avoiding the threads, too. They also put down flour.

At eleven p.m. the footsteps began again. At two a.m. a terrible series of cold airwaves swept through the house. The reporters said they felt the temperature drop from about 70 degrees to 40 degrees and everybody looked for sweaters and coats to keep warm. Mrs. Craighill smelled perfume. A check of the attic revealed no disturbance in the flour on the floor and no bells ever rang.

Ten-year-old Anne became hysterical and had to be taken away to the home of an aunt. Mrs. Craighill broke down and had to be sedated.

And now a new problem befell the unfortunate families. Since the appearance in the Telegram of the story about the Etobicoke ghost, the house was beseiged by the curious. The Bullens left the house, followed in a few hours by the Craighills, but still the mob gathered. It took four policemen to keep order.

The newsmen, in an attempt to trace the history of the house, interviewed William Tomlinson whose great-grandfather had built it. Mr. Tomlinson said his grandparents had lived in the house. Tomlinson himself bought it in 1942 and converted it into apartments. All that sounded quite ordinary. But Tomlinson also said that for last 15 years of his grandfather's life the upstairs was never used.

"I don't know why." Tomlinson said.

And so the newspaper dropped the story, the two families moved, and the furor died down.

The Bartletts, however, had their own theory. They still felt that the disturbance was caused by a thought form. It was found out that an elderly woman once lived in the house and was expert at fortune-telling. She became rather peculiar in old age, however, and took to sitting at the dormer window in the attic to shout songs at the passersby. Neighbors complained about the noise, and the woman was forced to move. She was alive at the time of the Craighill haunting, living some miles from the Etobicoke house. She had some idea that she was 'keeping the house for her son'.

Mr. Bartlett concluded that there was nothing to be afraid of in the attic.

"The poltergeist activity in that house was caused by the ghost form or thought form of a person not yet dead, but miles away, thinking about past experiences which she wanted to relive."

He theorized that the old woman was able to project her thought form back into the house where she once lived and that in a sense, she had returned there.

The idea of thought forms, and travelling out of the physical body is a very old one. The priests of Tibet were alleged to be particularly adept at this kind of supernormal activity. So it is possible that a powerful motivation might produce a similar effect when an untrained but possibly psychic western woman put her mind to the problem.

THE POLICEMAN AND THE POLTERGEIST

"I'm not sure what it's after, but it isn't me."

That's what Mrs. James Ackerman of Picton, Ontario had to say about the 'thing' in her attic. Looking at her photograph, one would expect any ghost or poltergeist to be intimidated. Mrs. Ackerman looked fascinating in the picture run by the Toronto Globe and Mail, but she did not look like a woman to trifle with. .

The noise in the attic didn't seem to know that. It didn't seem to be afraid of policemen either. The case ended on a rather uncertain note, but while it lasted it was a classic. There were points about it that were similar to the story of the attic noises in Etobicoke where the Craighills and the Bullens were under seige.

In August, 1939, Mrs. Ackerman occupied a large yellow frame house on Queen Street in Picton. Living with her were her young niece, Elda Brough (14) and her nephew, Willet Brough (20). They were awakened one night by a loud pounding on the door which sealed off the attic.

All three went up to the attic to look but found nothing. When it happened the next night, they told the neighbors. The neighbors called the police.

Constable John Armstrong answered the call.

He was a man of direct action. First he ordered everybody out of the house, then he turned off all the lights, and then with his flashlight in hand, he went to the attic.

"As I neared the attic door it sounded," Constable Armstrong reported afterwards, "Somebody with the flat of the hand on the other side of the door. I opened the door fast, shone my flashlight in. Nobody there. I searched the attic and found nothing."

Thinking it over, Constable Armstrong said,

"Now it's like this. I don't believe in ghosts but there's something funny about all this."

There was something funny, but nobody could get to the truth of the matter. Other officers investigated the disturbances and they were 'beaten too' according to Constable Armstrong.

Willet Brough drove a spike through the attic door to keep it shut. But the night after he did that both he and his sister were awakened again with the pounding on the door. Willet went up to investigate. He was standing in front of the door when he saw the knob turn slowly. Then the door flew open with a bang. The spike had been knocked out.

Since the house was fifty years old, it was checked for drafts and noisy pipes. No explanation for the noises and the door-opening could be found.

Two stories and a half-dozen photographs in the Toronto Globe and Mail, however, brought a crowd of curious people to the Ackerman house. Police had to be called to quell the disturbance. The Globe and Mail sent Ralph Allen (then a reporter but later to become editor of Maclean's Magazine, managing editor of the Toronto Daily Star and an author) to cover it. His front page story told of the crowds, the vigil and the lack of any noises from the attic. Evidently the sensation-seekers accomplished what the police, and the spike through the door could not do; they frightened off the poltergeist.

No explanation was ever found for the disturbances in the Ackerman house and the story simply faded into obscurity.

Chapter Five

HOW TO TALK TO A GHOST

PHOTOGRAPHS OF GHOSTS

In 50 Great Ghost Stories (1966), Ronald Seth states, "While apparitions have not yet been scientifically accounted for, the many authenticated ghost stories told for many centuries, and very widely believed, forbid any thinking person from declaring that there is nothing in it when haunted houses and the return of disembodied spirits are being discussed."

Those who seriously investigate psychic matters learn to respect, and even to dread at times, the vast unknown world whose occupants so desperately and consistently demand our recognition and understanding. We know so little about the supernatural that caution still plays a primary role in its researching. Curiosity and intellectual intrigue come a close second. At this stage, it is a bold, and occasionally foolish, man who will categorically deny the existence of such things as ghosts. Being personally involved in a single serious incident is usually all that is required to change the mind of such an individual.

Amongst the very intelligent and well-educated, amongst clergymen and rabid anti-clerics, you will encounter firm believers in psychic phenomena. There are no vocational, religious, sexual or educational barriers standing between those who are willing to learn more about the supernatural. These people are not gullible ; nor will they accept without argument and reasonable proof all that they are told. They are just more prepared to listen and consider, to debate and then reconsider. Their minds are receptive to new ideas.

Dedicated investigators check out the many reports of spectral sightings, and photographs have been obtained of some of the more famous and predictable apparitions. As modern science advances, it can be expected that the scientific proofs of spiritual manifestations will also increase in both substance and reliability. Already there is sufficient evidence to challenge any individual with an active mind.

As early as 1936, the December issue of the popular English magazine, *Country Life,* published a photograph which was destined to provoke a great deal of heated debate between those who accepted the existence of ghosts and those who denied them. Today, almost forty years later, the same arguments are being repeated.

The photograph purported to be an actual picture of the elusive Brown Lady of Raynham Hall in Norfolk, England. No hoax was ever uncovered. The photographer did not even believe in ghosts. He was utterly astonished when he first viewed the printed picture.

A man with an international reputation, he was on assignment to photograph the magnificent interior of Raynham Hall. In those days a crude form of flash was used to light indoor pictures and the resultant light could temporarily blind the photographer. On this occasion, the photographer had taken the picture without being aware of the apparition watching him from the top of the stairs.

The monks of Winchester Cathedral are a legend. Many people claim to have seen the ghostly figures but one man took a photograph of them.

In 1958, T.L. Taylor, an electrical engineer and 42 years of age, was visiting the Cathedral with his wife, his 16-year-old daughter and a friend. He took two pictures of the high altar on a 35 m.m. camera with color film.

In the first picture the choir stalls are empty. In the second picture taken about one minute later there are thirteen figures shown. The line of the altar's steps can be clearly seen through the transparent shapes. The figures wore robes or cloaks described as 'from Plantagenet or Tudor times'. One figure was bearded.

The color film was examined by experts and it was claimed that there was no double exposure. Taylor, apparently, was as surprised as anybody.

In 1962, a photograph was taken of a single ghost. This apparition was standing in the burned out ruins which are all that remain today of Ballyheigue Castle in Ireland.

Unfortunately, from the point of view of the ghost-seeker searching for just this sort of filmed proof, American and Canadian spirits would appear to be more camera-shy. Or perhaps it is just that they are more modern and camera-conscious. They might be deliberately preventing us from taking their pictures. Both indoor and night photography require careful and skilled advance preparations. And the ghosts involved are seldom co-operative enough to appear at just the right moment.

Photographs are not, of course, immune to accidental error or deliberate manipulation. But, while no concrete, unchallengeable evidence has been offered to prove the many tales of spectral appearances, there is a growing amount of filmed documentation indicating that these psychic apparitions are very real and can be quite visible when they so desire. We must allow, even expect, that there will be attempts to take advantage of the growing interest in ghosts. Still, it is quite remarkable that any such pictures exist in the first place. Just encountering a ghost is apt to render the strongest people weak-kneed and shakey-handed for a while.

In recent years, many of the better psychic investigators have reached the conclusion that particularly strong ghosts can be seen, felt, heard and tape-recorded. They can also be photographed by a skilled and reasonably shock-proof photographer.

If we can collect such technological evidences of supernatural and spiritual existence, it follows that there must be something quite real behind the various manifestations.

ONE SOLUTION

Not all mysterious stories about ghostly appearances go through history unsolved. Occasionally the accumulation of evidence leads the investigators to the conclusion that they are dealing with man-made ghosts. Some hauntings are undoubtedly the result of human attempts to conceal a secret, discourage tenancy or perpetuate a hoax. Others are invented for the sheer fun of fooling people and observing their varied reactions to unusual situations. Practical jokers love inventing ghosts. Hence we find the natural reluctance of the press to become involved with a reported sighting. And there have been enough falsified reports from publicity seekers and jokesters to justify this attitude of skepticism.

Paul Bloomfield (*Red Blood and Royal,* 1965) worked out a partial explanation for one of the not-so supernatural hauntings. For many years, apprehension and interest had surrounded the nature of the Strathmore heritage. This proud English family was incredibly rich and powerful.

Upon coming of age, each consecutive Strathmore heir was told some great and apparently fearful secret. None of these men ever betrayed the nature of this trust laid upon them. Over the years, all sorts of weird guesses were made concerning the possibly supernatural content of a tale which so obviously had to be kept carefully concealed from the outside world. What on earth were the Strathmores hiding? Only a very few trusted individuals knew the answer, and they said nothing to quell the rumors.

Bloomfield feels that he has solved the puzzle. He believes that, in this particular instance, the blue-blooded Strathmores were embarrassed. They were trying to conceal the existence of a mongoloid heir who should rightfully have inherited the vast lands. He was also entitled to the family leadership and title. Since this man survived into late adulthood, several heirs had to be told of his existence and subsequent incarceration within the family walls. It was obviously to their advantage to remain silent.

The aristocratic Strathmores must have felt that their proud family name and reputation should be protected from this physical "blemish" in their midst. A decision may have been made to let people continue thinking that they were being haunted by some spirit with an ancient grudge.

Since the Strathmore's wide holdings do have a history of violence, it is quite possible that there were also other evidences of spectral activities to justify the local speculation. Bloomfield's description of hiding an unfit heir in just peculiar enough to have actually happened. At any rate, the real nature of the Strathmore secret is still as much of a mystery today as it was long ago.

COMMUNICATION WITH GHOSTS

Methods of making contact with supernatural or spiritual beings are not restricted to the deliberate use of the ouija board. Frequently it is the spectre, not the human, who desires contact and takes the first step towards establishing a relationship. Ghosts have numerous ways of communicating with those who possess an abnormal awareness or a highly developed psychic sense. They employ automatic writing, disembodied voices, gestures, tapping codes, thought transference and simple dream messages. Sometimes they mix all the techniques together in order to create a desired effect.

None of these systems is foolproof. Still they have occasionally been effective when used by capable individuals who refuse to be frightened or disconcerted. By the utilization of these and other more personalized methods, some rather nasty hauntings have been cleared up.

What does the ghost want? The main problem of any haunting would appear to lie in an early and accurate determination of the purpose, if there is one, of the ghostly visitation. Some spirits just wish to be recognized. The seemingly simple act of recognition is a tacit admission on our part that there really is a world beyond the one in which we now dwell. Other ghosts need to relate or dramatize the tale of an ancient wrong. Some require verbal reassurance that an important matter has been settled to their satisfaction. Still others seem lost and in desperate need of direction. These latter ones just have to be firmly told that they are no longer required to remain on this particular plane.

BILINGUAL GHOSTS

Two Ontario ghost stories which are similar in many ways, illustrate a form of communication with spirits which seemed at the time each happened to be very casual. Both stories include a Frenchman returning to communicate with the living, and both have a young girl in the cast of characters.

Sixteen miles east of Belleville, Mrs. John Palmer occupied a four-roomed house on the Ticonderoga Reserve. Mrs. Palmer was 100 years old at the time of the occurrence and while some people might discount her as witness because of her extreme age, her daughter and son-in-law, Mr. and Mrs. Gerald Wahn, and their eleven-year-old daughter, Linda also testify to the events.

Mrs. Palmer described her frequent conversations with a long-dead Frenchman called Louis Carpentier, in this fashion :

"He starts knocking on my bedroom wall every night about eight and we talk back and forth."

The Wahns and Linda also talked to Louis. Linda said that Louis told her how card tricks were done and that she was not afraid of him.

"It's a ritual every night. We hear the knocking and it's Louis. We talk about all kinds of things." Gerald Wahn said.

Mrs. Palmer said that Louis told her he was robbed and murdered by Indians near her home in the early 1800's. He was on a timber buying trip from Montreal at the time. Louis refused to talk when strangers were present but he did knock sometimes to let them know Mrs. Palmer wasn't joking.

Altogether, seventeen neighbors heard Louis knock and signed a sworn statement to that effect. A contractor from Frankford, James Jones, said,

"I thought it was all bunk but I brought two friends

along and we heard him rap out 'there are three strangers in the house'."

Quite a bit of Louis' conversation appears to have been a repetition of what went on in the house all day. This must have been rather boring. One wishes Mrs. Palmer and her relatives had asked Louis some pointed questions about the 'other side' and life in Canada in the early part of the nineteenth century.

Louis would go on, apparently, until the family got tired of talking to him and then they told him to go to bed. He was very obedient and stopped talking until the next night.

There are many aspects of this story which make one wish that a qualified investigator had looked into the matter. Did Louis speak French or English? There is no information about that, or whether he spoke some kind of universal language which everybody could easily understand. When Louis rapped out a message as he did for Mr. Jones, how was it translated? Was the Morse code used, and if so, did everybody there understand the Morse code?

A similar tale emerged in 1952 from a small village called Swastika, five miles west of Kirkland Lake, Ontario. The family involved was that of Aime Desmarthais, and they were completely French-speaking.

Much of the activity seems to have centered around twelve-year-old Lucienne. It began with a knocking in the roof of the Desmarthais house. An investigation revealed no cause for the knocking. The knocking then moved to the floor of an upstairs bedroom. Thinking an animal might somehow be trapped there, the family had the floor of the bedroom torn up but found nothing.

Then the noises began to follow Lucienne from room to room. A voice spoke to her in French. With witnesses present. Lucienne talked to the ghost. She asked it to rap once if it was her grandfather who had died four months earlier. A single rap was the response. Despite this, the family moved out of the house.

A neighbor, Mrs. Lomer Lamothe was so impressed with the rappings that she suggested calling in the American Society of Psychical Research to investigate the whole affair in a proper manner. Apparently nothing was done about this as there is no record of anything further being discovered.

Again as in the Belleville story, we have a mixture of rapping and 'speaking French' so that it is not clear from the records whether the ghost chose his method of communication at random, and whether the rappings were in some code which everybody understood. In the Desmarthais story nobody enquired why the grandfather had come back, apparently. What did he want? What did he have to report about his own restless state? If it was truly the grandfather, one would expect the family to accept him as a benign spirit and remain in the house, yet the published story says the family moved out.

Many people believe in reincarnation, even today. In spite of its antiquity as a concept, reincarnation has a lot to offer in a distressed atomic age. Besides the promise of life after death, reincarnation is based on a certain logic. Almost every human has asked himself at some time, why some men starve and others are overfed, why some men are ugly and some are handsome, some sick and others well.

The theory of reincarnation explains away these injustices. You are suffering because you made mistakes in an earlier life, or conversely, you are successful because you made so much progress in an earlier life.

"All ancient peoples, including the Egyptians," says James Churchward, author of the currently popular Mu books, "believed in the reincarnation of the soul!"

Churchward was a geologist and anthropologist who became obsessed with the history of man, which began according to him on the Lost Continent of Mu. Mu was located in the Pacific Ocean. The Lost Continent of Atlantis was a colony of Mu.

In the Lost Continent of Mu, Churchward quotes an Egyptian source, *Papyrus Anana:*

"Men do not live once only and then depart hence forever. They live many times in many places, although not always on this world. Between each life there is a veil of darkness."

Why does man's spirit keep returning to Earth? Because, say the believers, he is struggling to perfect his soul so that he may finally join the Supreme Being in the spirit world and live there forever in bliss. And that's where Karma comes in. Karma is the soul's debt which it carries from life to life. You reap what you sow. Karma is like a cosmic abacus, toting up your good deeds and your bad deeds. You will have to pay off those bad deeds in some other life and it may be uncomfortable for you. That's why it is sensible to be good in *this* life.

The American psychic, Edgar Cayce was a devout and orthodox Protestant. He had read the Bible once for each of his forty-six years when in August, 1923, while in deep trance, he stated emphatically that the law of reincarnation was a fact. Later, when he awoke and was told what he had said, Cayce was shocked.

As he continued to give readings while in trance, Cayce talked more and more about the previous lives of the subjects who had come to him for help. He came to believe implicity in reincarnation.

"When a soul enters a new body," Cayce explained, "a door is opened, leading to an opportunity for building the soul's destiny."

Cayce also believed that Christ taught reincarnation as part of his own religious outlook. In his book, "Edgar Cayce on Reincarnation", Noel Langley devotes a whole chapter to the theory that references to reincarnation were taken out of the Bible deliberately and that the impetus for this was given by Emperor Justinian in 553 A. D. through the Fifth Ecumenical Congress of Constantinople.

The argument about reincarnation has gone on through the ages and will no doubt continue to go on for many ages to come. It is such a difficult concept for most people to understand that they may want to reject it completely just as they are at a loss when it comes to handling the various problems presented by a supernatural manifestation.

An accomplished seer or medium, such as Sybil Leek, can sometimes intercept critical communications from spirits. The average individual may find it too difficult, but a seer can help by translating the messages from beyond into the desired action or response.

A reminder should be included at this point. Intercession between the living and the dead is not an easy task; nor should it be undertaken lightly or without a very real need. If you do not know anything about communication with ghosts, do not attempt to act as a casual interpreter of their messages. An ordinary individual should stay completely clear of serious involvement in such affairs. The result of an error on your part could be most unpleasant, and might hinder rather than aid troubled spirits. The idea is to help them; we should not utilize their presence for personal reasons. To increase their confusion, even unintentionally, would be cruel and pointless.

But, approached rationally and calmly, communications can be effectively established between the living and the dead. There are many recorded incidents of help or warning being passed on to living humans by those now dwelling "on the other side". Such messages should be heeded; they can be very important.

A relative or good friend may see the concerned individual at the moment of, or shortly after, that person's physical death in another location. Frequently the visit is accompanied by unexpected help or instruction. Some ghosts appear solely to protect friends or relatives from unseen danger. Others merely want to reassure those who have been left behind. They may reveal something as crucial as a secret place where they have been hiding emergency-money which will be required now for the support of the family.

A ghost can be a perfect stranger. Up until fairly recently, it was believed that the assistance offered by spirits to humans was confined to those who had known and loved them in the past. In fact, spectres have appeared to aid complete strangers who needed their gift of foreknowledge.

WHO WILL SEE A GHOST ?

There can be little doubt that some people are more susceptible than others to feelings, sensations, sightings and messages from the past and future. This is not as complicated as it may seem at first. They are simply more aware of what is going on around them. Naturally enough, this heightened awareness has led to their being called "sensitives".

These receptive individuals are sometimes said to possess the sixth sense or second sight. We usually call them "psychics". Occasionally they have been able to act as intermediaries between those in the world of the living and those who inhabit the spirit levels beyond our comprehension. A less acute individual might not like a house or an area. He might feel, "There is something wrong; something's the matter with this place". A person with a highly developed psychic sense may be able to locate the source of the difficulty and actually eliminate the problem through communication with the unknown spirit causing the trouble.

A psychic may see ghosts and be able to understand them. But such communication is a risky business at best.

The physical phenomena of mediumship are known to impose a heavy strain on both mind and body. Even under medically controlled conditions, electrocardiogram and electroencephalograph tests change markedly when a person slips into a physical trance of any depth. Bleeding is noticeably reduced. There is no response to painful stimuli. When an unknown spirit guide takes over a human body in order to communicate, the human involved even shows a variation in his responses to pretested drugs. In short, the body is no longer that of the medium. For the moment at least, it is being controlled by a totally different being.

The effect of these major physical alternations is difficult to determine, but one thing is very clear. An untrained or nervous individual would be ill-advised, if not downright foolish, to become involved in mediumistic aspects of the supernatural.

A School for Mediums does exist. It is available for those who feel that they simply must utilize their sensitivity. This training centre is in London, England, along with several other agencies that investigate reports of psychic events.

The curriculum at the School for Mediums is a demanding one. People who are naturally psychic or receptive are taught what has been learned to date about the various methods of communication needed to deal with the spirits about them. They develop their mediumistic powers and practice extreme self-control. They strengthen those types of thought transference which will enable them to work efficiently, effectively and safely with some of the supernatural elements they may encounter. In a way, this course could be interpreted as being one dealing primarily with mental self-defence.

Animals are reported to have a far greater sensitivity to the presence of ghosts than the average human. This should not come as too much of a surprise. For years,

dogs have been used to track or find what we were unable
to locate with our limited sensory development. We have
long been aware that their abilities to hear and smell
are more highly developed than our own. Their other
senses may also differ in some less evident, but equally
important way.

Animals will often see or sense the presence of an
apparition long before the less aware human being senses
anything unusual in his surroundings. Horses refuse to
pass by certain areas at night. Dogs will suddenly cringe
or begin to wail dismally for no apparent reason. The
alertness and uneasy mannerisms of cats, dogs and horses
have frequently been the first indication of a forthcoming
supernatural manifestation. Their purely instinctive actions
and reactions can scarcely be blamed upon prior knowledge of the unusual historical background of a specific
house. Humans are indeed susceptible to such psycholo-
gical influences — animals are not.

Cats have been associated with the supernatural for
generations in many different countries. Egyptian royalty
pampered these animals as good luck charms or spirits.
And it was once believed here, not so long ago, that cats
acted as messengers or mediums for workers of witchcraft. The charge was false, we now believe, but the idea
still persists. Some people continue to regard ordinary
domestic cats with an awe and respect to which they are
not truly entitled. It is acknowledged that there is something most peculiar about feline independence, but this
has little or nothing to do with unnatural phenomena.

Children, too, are frequently credited with an innate
ability for contacting spiritual beings. Perhaps this is
because they are less skeptical, more willing to accept
things at face value. It is not necessary for them to apply
past readings and teachings to each new experience. They
are less apt to criticize the evidence of their own senses.
Only later, over the years, does adult skepticism gain
ascendance.

Small children have been known to see ghosts and to speak quite calmly to them. Apparently they notice nothing frightening or unusual about these incidents. Many parents describe how their children have "invented" invisible playmates with whom they spend many enjoyable hours. It is just possible that some of these imaginary children are small, lonely spirits accepted by our youngsters and not even seen by the rest of us.

Chapter Six

SPIRITS OF QUEBEC

JOHANNE

A child will often accept evidence of the supernatural while the adults around her become excited and skeptical. Johanne Allison, an eight-year-old living in Lower Town, Quebec, reported one day that she had seen a vision of her late mother. Instead of invoking a calm and interested reaction, Johanne found that her simple statement brought chaos and hysteria to her friends and relatives.

On September 18, 1967, Johanne visited the Notre-Dame-de-Grace Roman Catholic Church in Lower Town, Quebec. There was nothing unusual about this ; she had done the same thing many times before.

After leaving the main church buildings, Johanne entered the small Grotto which lies behind the central structure. There she claims to have made three wishes. And they do sound quite typical of the requests that might be made by an eight-year-old. She wished to see her mother again, to receive a bicycle of her very own for a present, and for her father to become a wealthy man.

It was at this point, just after making her wishes, that Johanne saw a vision of her late mother. Mrs. Allison had died about a year and a half prior to the incident. According to Alexandre Allison, the girl's father, Johanne had been praying regularly in the Grotto since the death of her mother.

Johanne claims that the face of her mother appeared beside a statue of the Virgin Mary. This piece of statuary stands inside the Grotto itself, and it later proved to be the focal point of much of the confusion.

The child's pleased and excited report to her friends and family resulted in a form of mass hysteria which eventually spread throughout the entire neighborhood. Her young classmates misinterpreted her statement. They thought she was claiming to have seen the Virgin Mary. Thousands of people flocked hopefully to the Grotto in the days that followed. The little statue was completely covered with offerings of bright flowers and rosaries.

The following weekend, September 25, the road leading to the Grotto was blocked by people. Many fainted and had to be treated for hysteria and heat prostration. Reporters noticed that there were no priests or nuns in the vast crowd. It consisted of a surprisingly large number of teenagers. There were as many men as women. One dominant group were members of the Pilgrims for a Better World, a political organization which advocates Social Credit doctrine and is commonly known as the "White Berets".

Johanne's father, an employee of the Canadian National Railroads, was forced to move his family out of the district. It was the only way for them to get some respite from the constant commotion engendered by the misinterpreted sighting.

Although subjected to many detailed questions by the local clerical authorities and by members of her own immediate family, the bewildered girl held her ground. Johanne maintained that her mother appeared as if in direct response to her wish. She was not afraid, and could not understand why all the adults were so upset.

Perhaps, in the Allison case, a kindly and well-meaning spirit was warmly and calmly received by her lonely child. On the other hand, a malevolent manifestation will cause the same sort of mindless terror in a youngster as is found in animals encountering phenomena linked with the world of the supernatural. The instincts of children and animals are fairly dependable.

Johanne probably made it easy for her mother to return because of her uncomplicated receptiveness to the idea. She may be slightly psychic. It is quite possible that this child will have other experiences related to the supernatural for the same reason. Her openness and trust make her a good receiver.

The only widely publicized clerical comment on the Allison incident came from Reverend Raymond Lavoie, priest of a neighboring parish. Most of the other church leaders were unwilling to commit themselves. Reverend Lavoie stated that, "God usually manifests Himself by supernatural signs such as apparitions in areas where faith has become feeble and decadent. In this region, I believe that the level of faith is sufficiently feeble, but one must be prudent about saying that there has been an apparition."

THE INVISIBLE CAT

A Canadian family living at the present time in Montreal has a most peculiar problem. Brian and Louise

Grey have simply come to accept it as a part of their daily existence over the past few years. Although this family, which includes four children, does not own a cat, there is definitely such an animal living in the house with them. This would be acceptable except for one small detail. The cat has been heard and it has been felt. No one has ever seen this cat.

The first visit of this feline spirit took place late one afternoon in the master bedroom. The bedroom is located on the second floor of the two-storey residence. The lady of the house, Louise Grey, had experienced a trying day. She was stretched out on her bed resting quietly before tackling the dinner preparations. Then, she felt the slight "plop" that cats apparently make when they land on top of a bed.

The door of the master bedroom was completely closed. There was really no way for an ordinary cat to have entered the room.

Mrs. Grey lay quite still, thinking that perhaps her children had played a trick upon her. She thought that she might have dozed off just long enough for them to slip a stray cat into the room.

The cat walked slowly across the bed towards the window. Still, Louise Grey could not bring herself to roll over and watch its progress. She has no explanation for this lack of motion other than that she seemed to sense that something was wrong.

Then, Mrs. Grey felt the bed move slightly in recoil as the cat leaped across to the windowsill. She flipped over, and simply stared in amazement. There was no cat in the casement window. Nor could it have left through the window. While the window itself was open, the screen was still firmly in place. Besides, even a cat might hesitate before jumping from a second-storey window onto a concrete patio below.

After that, the cat came back frequently. Apparently spirit-cats are not so different from ordinary cats; they find a place where they can maintain a high degree of independence and then settle right in to make themselves at home.

Tom Grey, a third-year university student, had been away at school when the cat moved into the house. His mother wrote him about the incident and he responded with a note reflecting disbelief. When Tom came home for vacation, he was met by his excited brother and sisters. They hurried to confirm the strange story.

Tom refused to believe what he was hearing, even when his mother supplied further details about her experience. And, skeptical about the supernatural, Tom determined to see this cat and disprove the family's theories regarding invisibility of animals.

Early one summer morning, the disbelieving young student got a first-hand opportunity to test his theory. He experienced a visit from the elusive cat. Tom felt the animal land right on the small of his back while he lay in bed. The weight seemed about right for a cat. Tom played possum, tensing himself to spring suddenly in order to catch the animal.

Moments passed. The cat walked right up to the head of the bed, brushing lightly against the boy's hair. It crossed over the pillow and settled down beside Tom's left ear. He could even hear the sound of gentle purring.

But, when the youth raised his head and looked at where the cat should have been, there was nothing to be seen. He could still hear the soft purring next to his pillow. And the pillow itself was flattened as though something were lying against it.

Now the invisible cat is an accepted member of the family. It causes no trouble, costs nothing to feed, and is missed when it does not turn up for several days.

When I asked the owner of this unusual cat if she believed in the existence of ghosts, I fully expected a positive response. I was wrong. She thought for a moment before replying;

"No. Not really. I believe that sometimes when you

are thinking about someone you were once very fond of, then there is a sort of feeling of closeness that is almost a spiritual experience in itself. But my only personal contact with that kind of thing has been in connection with that cat of ours. We have never been able to figure out how to explain it properly. Funny things just happen, I guess".

ST. BRUNO

A religious manifestation was reported from Quebec in July of 1968. Despite the natural reluctance of experienced religious authorities to encourage the emotionalism surrounding such events, this incident was fully covered by the news media.

The initial experience occurred in a large, muddy, open field in St. Bruno. This is a small town situated about fifteen miles to the south of greater Montreal.

Six girls, ranging in age from four to thirteen, were involved in the actual sighting. They claimed that the Virgin Mary appeared before them on July 22 while they were walking in the field. There were just enough minor inconsistencies in their individual stories to give the whole episode a certain ring of truth. Six children of such varying ages would certainly have noticed different details. It would have been far more suspicious if they had all said the same thing during the ensuing interviews.

The girls maintained that they saw the Virgin between two clouds. She was wearing a long white gown, a white veil and a blue mantle. The mantle was covered with innumerable stars. Two of the older girls mustered up their courage and spoke to the vision. They were apparently told that she would appear before them again on October 7. The strange appointment was set for about the same time of day. The Virgin was to appear at dusk.

No reason was offered for the appearance of the apparition or for that particular choice of a return date. Nor did the vision explain why she was planning to return to St. Bruno. She then disappeared into the growing dusk while a large choir of angels sang, "Gloria, gloria." Or so the children unanimously claimed.

Before discounting this story as a childish prank that simply got out of hand, one should consider that these children were brought up to respect the church and its officers. Religion was an integral part of their daily lives. The older ones would have been aware of the consequences, the punishments and loss of face, if they were found to be lying about having seen the Virgin. The smaller children probably would have confessed quickly to a falsehood when faced with parental doubts and questioning. Their statements did not alter following the incident.

During the next few months, more than twenty people came forward to report that they, too, had seen this vision or another form of the same apparition. On October 7, over 20,000 people gathered in the field in the cold, drizzling rain. Highway Number 9 was blocked for hours by parked and stalled vehicles.

The motives of the crowd were mixed. They ranged from curiosity to a wish to be blessed, from the urge to laugh at the others gathered there to the desperate hope to be cured of some serious ailment. Believers and nonbelievers, Catholics and non-Catholics, gathered together in the rain. Many of those who ridiculed the watchers had visited the local tavern before going to the site.

The Virgin did not appear on the designated evening. The vast crowd and the hopeful television crews waited in vain. Several individuals thought that they saw her, but most of the people went away disappointed. Many of them had driven for miles in order to be present. Ohio, New York, Massachusetts and California license plates were seen. Two bus loads from Boston were in attendance that night.

Despite the failure of the vision to appear, the belief of some of the individuals was not weakened. One man said, "I do believe she did appear to the little girls. She may have her own reason if she does not appear tonight".

He added thoughtfully, "It is not for human beings to judge such things".

At present, the man is quite right about our inability to assign motives to supernatural manifestations. But, perhaps one day soon, humans will be in a better position to evaluate such matters. Our slowly developing knowledge should lead us to the understanding we seek with regard to all of the supernatural phenomena. This, in turn, may prove to be the crucial turning point. It will help us to prevent hoaxes and mass hysteria. And, we will be better able to differentiate between actual events and mere coincidence and suggestibility.

Following the unproductive evening at St. Bruno, Mrs. Leo St. Jean, mother of three of the girls present during the original manifestation, collapsed and was hospitalized. One of her daughters was treated for nervous exhaustion.

Provincial and St. Bruno police remained on duty with local firemen until early in the morning of September 8. It was not until then that the crowd began to break up and head for home. Some still refused to leave; they planned to stay for the remainder of the night.

This manifestation, if that is what it was, had one interesting result. It showed the power of faith and hope to move people towards accepting unusual events.

GUYLAINE

A single bizarre occurrence took place in Acton Vale, Quebec, about sixty-five miles from Montreal. It reveals the mixed results that can arise from the attempted exorcism of an unfriendly supernatural manifestation. It also illustrates quite clearly the emotional confusion surrounding such unnatural incidents and the people who suddenly find themselves involved.

The series of events took place one day in January of 1969. They happened in the home of the Saint-Onges family. Guylaine, a six-year-old child boarding at the

Saint-Onges, and assorted religious and personal objects became the centre of a most unusual performance.

A sacred painting, although attached securely to the wall, started things off. It suddenly flew down the length of the room to the doorknob. Then it jumped to a nearby dresser and to the floor where it began to enact a weird sort of rhythmic dancing pattern.

The Saint-Onges family watched in horror.

Beds were stripped of their linen and torn apart by something that no one could see or control. Mattresses were tossed about the house as if by a powerful and utterly insane force. The Saint-Onges stubbornly remade their beds, which promptly and defiantly flew apart again.

Little Guylaine seemed to be the focal point of this frightening and violent turmoil. She was trying in vain to dress for her morning classes. Her clothes danced about her. An array of rosaries, ash-trays and vases filled the air in her vicinity. Mrs. Saint-Onges handed a rosary to the child. She hoped that this religious symbol might stop or at least reduce the commotion. Guylaine was unable to retain the rosary. Something unseen snatched it right out of her small hands.

Help was obviously needed. Three priests, Abbé Claude Léveillé, Abbé Normand Bernier and Abbé Wilfrid Bérard, were called in. They watched for a while and promised to try to aid the beseiged family.

The clergymen began by sprinkling holy water liberally about the room which appeared to be the most critically affected. Next they tried to exorcise the spirit. Initially, the exorcism seemed to be totally ineffective. The thing had no intention of being removed so easily. A table and two religious statues were broken in the upsurge of mindless violence.

Eventually, several hours later, peace was restored. Whether or not this was as a result of the exorcism is a matter for debate. The three priests left, promising to issue a detailed statement explaining their interpretation of the peculiar incident.

The trio of clergymen took well over a week to consider the matter. Perhaps they required the time to consult with their superiors. There may have been no one in their parish or immediate vicinity with experience in exorcisms. But the priests could not deny the story; they had personally witnessed the invasion of the Saint-Onges home. Local residents and the national press were waiting to see how the matter would be resolved.

Finally the priests issued a statement that reads in part; "It is the case of a diabolical phenomenon ... he always attacks holy things and seems to fear their use against him ... the first thing to do was search for possible natural causes but it was quickly established that there was no vibration on the walls, there was no draft and no one was touching the articles ... those who were in the house began to pray and things quieted down."

The priests concluded, "We believe that the message that God wanted to transmit to Acton Vale was transmitted. The supernatural exists, even if our scientific spirit leads us to doubt it, and we are invited to better observe our faith and to pray more and more for sinners".

Following the statement made by the clergymen, no further incidents were reported by the Saint-Onges family. There are two possible reasons, either of which could account for this result. The exorcism conducted in Acton Vale may have been successful despite the initial delay. It may have gotten rid of the anti-religious spirit that was persecuting Guylaine. On the other hand, we cannot be sure that the source of this disturbance did not simply leave of its own accord.

It is interesting to speculate how this particular trouble-maker would react if he knew the reasons that had been attributed to his destructive performance. It seems unlikely that his initial aim, if indeed there was one, was to increase prayer and church attendance within the community. Unfortunately communication with this sort of entity is almost impossible.

Guylaine's parents took her way. Ignoring the verdict of the priests, they claimed that the child's vivid imagination was responsible for the incident. The Saint-Onges, with whom Guylaine had lived since she was a baby, disagreed. It was, and still is, their belief that the girl was a victim of some sort of devilish force.

A similar episode in another small Quebec town did not have such a satisfactory ending. In the early nineteen-sixties, a poltergeist drove an entire family of seven out of their home. The noise of banging cupboard doors and smashing china simply became too much to endure. The family asked the local church to help.

The parish priest who attempted the exorcism in this case was relatively new at the work. He had never performed an exorcism before and was afraid of his invisible antagonist. This fear and weakness must have showed.

In the middle of the exorcism rite there was an unexpected interruption. The angry and clearly unrepentant spirit threw an orange directly at the unfortunate clergyman. The poor fellow received a nasty black eye. For more than a week, he had to walk about the town with the mark of his battle clearly printed upon his face.

The poltergeist left the house about a week after the family members were forced to leave and two days after the exorcism. We will never be certain if the clergyman forced his departure or he just missed an audience for his antics.

Chapter Seven

POLTERGEISTS

OTHERS

"The ordinary ghost, although often inconsiderate, clumsy, noisy and frightening, is generally considered to be inoffensive, and even friendly and well-disposed to the living persons who occupy its place of haunting". This definition (Frank Usher in *50 Great Ghost Stories*) is acceptable if one keeps firmly in mind that the entity being discussed is an "ordinary" ghost.

But it is always dangerous to generalize with respect to either the motivational or behavioral patterns of ghosts. We simply do not know enough about them. Certainly there are some friendly, cooperative and playful spirits, although even the best of them can upset a family group just by its presence. There are also ghosts who are complete stinkers and cause nothing but trouble. Not many Canadian families would go so far as to actually welcome a ghost as a permanent, non-paying house guest.

There are other unnatural things besides ghosts. There are some completely malevolent forces that seem to exist for no other reason than to cause chaos, embarrassment and damage. And these are the ones that create the most concern in the minds of investigators of the supernatural.

In a famous and well-documented case, The Amherst Mystery of Nova Scotia, the spirit was held responsible for physical illnesses and mental breakdowns. It caused severe injuries to both humans and animals. The primary target of this spirit was a woman who was quite literally chased about the area.

The Amherst poltergeist was even blamed for a rash of large fires that suddenly broke out in the vicinity of the haunting. The vicious pranks were all of a very serious nature. This, the difference between mischievousness and unadulterated hatefulness, is the separation line that lies between the average ghost and the poltergeist.

The Amherst case took place a long time ago. Many books were written about it, and it is still used for comparative purposes by modern ghost-hunters and other seekers of supernatural phenomena.

Things do not seem to have changed much over the intervening years. Today Canada has just as many nasty incidents caused by evil spirits. We refer to these entities en masse as "poltergeists". These are far different from ordinary ghosts; nor is there anything the least bit funny about a visit from one. The violence of such infestations reaches a point where even the bravest and most stubborn individuals find it expedient to seek some sort of assistance. Sometimes they will do anything, try anything, in order to get relief.

A QUIET APPARITION

A quiet apparition might possibly be accepted or tolerated by a broad-minded family. This would eliminate the necessity of their having to confide in neighbors or the local authorities. Here, the ghosthunter is at a severe disadvantage. The haunting is isolated and kept secret from all except the immediate family members and a few trusted friends.

A poltergeist, on the other hand, is considered fair game. It can cause sufficient damage to justify a full-scale investigation. For the immediate sanity of those involved, it is usually customary to begin by checking with utility experts. They try to determine if the trouble could be the result of natural causes.

By this point, it is generally conceded that the people are dealing with some aspect of the supernatural but natural causes must be officially eliminated. If no land faults, plumbing failures or overloaded circuits turn up, the people involved begin to get desperate. Their next step may involve members of the clergy and a subsequent attempt to exorcise the visiting spirit. From these two primary sources, utility-men and clerics, stories of the activities of poltergeists find their way through the press and grapevine to a fascinated public.

Poltergeists, the most unpleasant of all psychic phenomena to date, appear unconcerned or merely angered at the showing of the Cross and the recitation of exorcism rites. They are seldom identified, or even personified to the extent of determining their sexual nature. Most people refer to all poltergeists as if they were either asexual or masculine. Reports will read, "He then threw things around the room ; he smashed up every bit of our good china too," or "It makes awful banging noises and keeps us awake during the night. I think it does it on purpose."

Some people contend that poltergeists are spirits of persons who died in a weakened condition and are thereby unable to express themselves through the more acceptable modes of communication. This is strictly theoretical ; it has yet to be verified. One point against this theory is that it does not account for the violence and nastiness found in so many of the poltergeist case histories.

The manifestation of a poltergeist is comparable to a sudden, explosive, energy discharge by a rather fiendish and frequently disagreeable intelligence source. Innocent individuals, often children, have been persecuted and severely injured by these things. And a poltergeist is capable of following its unwilling victim from one place to another. Whereas ghosts are generally associated with a particular area or dwelling, poltergeists attach themselves like leeches to specific persons or families. Only on rare occasions do they settle upon a definite place of operations.

Poltergeists are incredibly powerful. They can transport a body or article through the air with apparent ease regardless of its weight, size or shape. Chairs can be elevated despite the fact that someone quite solid might be sitting upon them at the time. Cupboard doors bang. Windows open and shut at odd and usually unappropriate moments.

A COW ON THE ROOF

One of the most frequent and frustrating pranks is the placing of a large and bulky animal in a normally inaccessible spot. Can you imagine the shocked and frightened reaction of the average farmer upon finding his prize bull has somehow gotten up into the barn's loft ? Added to the initial trauma is the problem of getting the creature back where it belongs.

People have also been bodily moved from place to place, and smashing massive objects into pieces is another undesirable trick of the poltergeist.

There was once a determined poltergeist at Christchurch in the island of Barbadoes. He, or it, spent several years repeatedly scrambling the coffins within a sealed family vault. No human being could have gained access. But, each time the vault had to be unsealed, the coffins were found in great confusion. They were turned on end and flung far from their original resting places.

The Barbados incident was thoroughly, but unsuccessfully, investigated. No natural cause was ever found. All that could be determined for certain was that ordinary vandals had not caused the damage. The vault is now empty and is left permanently open. No member of the family is even remotely interested in using it.

In the records, this is just another case of a poltergeist animated by a destructiveness and spite that seems utterly lacking in purpose and aim. Why would a force want to disturb a burial place? It doesn't make sense to the human mind and it may be some time before we can understand the weird motivation behind such an act.

The scrambling of the coffins did have one positive result. It showed beyond doubt that a poltergeist can operate without utilizing a living human being as a source of energy.

Children are often involved, directly or indirectly, in the background of investigations into poltergeists. In fact, at one time it was believed that such forces could operate only when there were children present in the area to serve as mediums or energy sources. This theory had been discarded, but it used to work out quite nicely for the poltergeist. The child could be blamed for the senseless destruction and violence.

In view of later evidence, it would appear that some children can, in an unconscious and uncontrolled way, increase the activity of certain poltergeists. They serve as unwilling assistants through which the entity gains additional power.

Children are not the only ones who find themselves embroiled with poltergeists. Fully grown adults have also served as highly reluctant mediums.

After going over all of the unappetizing poltergeistic characteristics, one fact becomes undeniably clear. A poltergeist is a nightmare come true. Anyone who asks you if he has a poltergeist operating in his home should probably be answered in the negative. If he had one, he would know it. A person posing that sort of question is more apt to have a plain ordinary everyday ghost on his hands. At the very worst, it could be a poltergeist in the earliest stages of development.

Chapter Eight

MORE ONTARIO GHOSTS

ST. CATHARINES

In February of 1970, strange reports began to come from St. Catharines, Ontario. They dealt with a ghostly force that was apparently being directed against the person of an eleven-year-old boy.

Bill and Marsha Walker (not their real names) had lived with their son, Peter, in a Church Street apartment for ten years. They had never experienced any trouble before. Now something or somebody, they didn't know which, was attacking young Peter.

The incidents took place only when the boy was in the

family's second-floor apartment. He seemed to act as an unwilling catalyst for the poltergeist whose activities were approaching frightening levels of violence.

A bed on which the boy was sleeping rose off the floor and then tipped onto its edge. He was dumped onto the floor with a resounding thud. A heavy chair in which he was sitting floated about seven inches off the floor while the family and friends watched in silent horror. The chair then suddenly overturned, trapping the youth firmly and violently against the near wall.

Policemen, lawyers, doctors, priests and laymen became involved in this psychic commotion. They all came to offer their help when the desperate family appealed for any and all available assistance. The Walkers were afraid that Peter would be badly hurt.

The cause of this disturbance was not at all reticent about performing when there were people in the apartment. If anything, he was a show-off. Furniture moved across the room, and doors suddenly opened although nobody had touched their knobs.

All the people there found themselves witnesses to a classic supernatural manifestation. Each reacted according to his individual personality, but most were forced to revise their thinking about evil spirits. It was a tough initiation for some of them. They did not want to believe that the thing annoying the boy was real, but the evidence of their senses was overwhelming.

The spirit seemed to know exactly which of his antics would most impress and frighten the spectators. The evidence indicated the presence of more cunning than reasoned intelligence. Perhaps the poltergeist felt there was some humor in his activities; the humans present did not. They were badly upset.

Witnesses who were determined to solve the mystery tried to find a natural cause, some sort of rational explanation that might account for the weird events. Inspectors from the various utility companies were called in for consultation. They failed to find a logical reason for the disturbance.

The Right Reverend Thomas J. McCarthy, Roman Catholic Bishop of St. Catharines, was informed about the trouble by two of his parish priests. He questioned them carefully before committing himself.

"I don't think there is any trickery. A lot of things happen that haven't been explained."

A constable who witnessed some of the irrational activities found himself in a moral dilemma. Being on duty at the time, he was supposed to write a report detailing everything he had seen. The constable, who wishes to remain unidentified, did not turn in the required description of his experience.

"Everyone would have thought I was crazy!"

The policeman need not have worried .There were plenty of other people involved in this incident who felt exactly the same way.

We may never know how the St. Catharines affair really ended. The family eventually had to refuse to allow any further investigations in their apartment. They were reported to have gone to Montreal on an extended visit.

There were no follow-up incidents after the initial Church Street problem, so perhaps the spirit has accomplished its strange purpose. There is no sane or reasonable explanation for what happened within our limited terms of reference. The Bishop's knowledge of the Walkers' problem suggest that a successful exorcism may have been conducted to help the boy and his family. I hope so for their sake.

THE SCREAMING WOMAN

In Hamilton, Ontario, a screaming ghost made a house on Brucedale Avenue uninhabitable. The house is gone now, a victim of the wrecker's ball, but the memory of it lingers on.

Mrs. Janice Bryant (not her real name) lived near a house with a peculiar history. She tells the story this way:

"It was in the early 1950's. That's when it all began. A couple of newlyweds moved into the house and as it turned out, they fought day and night. It was an awful marriage. Everyone around here complained about their shouting, and you could hear the sound of breaking china and glass almost every evening. Sometimes we couldn't get to sleep."

This went on for months, evidently, and then one night after a particularly violent quarrel, Mrs. Bryant heard an ambulance screech to a stop at the front door of the house. The young wife was removed on a stretcher.

"Later, we heard she died falling down the cellar stairs. They said it was an accident." Mrs. Bryant goes on, "But most of us thought she might have been pushed when they were fighting. Things got pretty rough in that house."

Shortly after the death, the husband placed the house on the market and moved away from the neighbourhood. A series of owners now began to live in the house. But nobody stayed for long.

"Every new owner had the same experience." Mrs. Bryant relates, "They'd hear these terrible screams in the night. A woman, obviously, but really chilling. All who heard the screams said they came from the cellar. They were convinced that the house was being haunted by a female spirit."

Some attempt was made to render the house fit for human habitation. A Roman Catholic priest was called in and an exorcism service conducted. His attempt was met with failure. The screaming continued.

Owners came and went; none remained for any length of time. So many reports of the ghostly screaming were made that the last set of owners decided to wreck the house. In the early 1960's, it was still in excellent condition, but no one could live in it.

A building contractor was called in. He and his men systematically tore this house right down to its foundation. A new one stands in its place today. So far, there are no fresh reports of screaming in the night.

This case illustrates the common theory that some people who die violently and suddenly refuse to admit that they are dead. They are frequently responsible for quite spectacular hauntings in or near their former residences.

RALPH

Ouija boards have long been recognized as adequate but fallible methods for communication with spirits. They can be easily manipulated by one or more of the individuals involved in the session. Sometimes the manipulation is totally unconscious and all those present will deny influencing the direction of the pointer.

In the Scarborough, Ontario, home of Mark and Helen Carson an invisible ghost came to visit in 1970. He took over their Lawrence Avenue East town house in a desperate attempt to avenge his alleged death at the hand of an unidentified assailant. It took a session on the ouija board to establish the ghost's aim.

Prior to the ouija board communication, the Carson household was disturbed by various unusual incidents.

"We have been hearing the sound of footsteps at night for several months now," said Mrs. Carson. "The doors open and close even when nobody is anywhere near them. The lights are turned on and off at the oddest times. And silly little things are mysteriously moved from one place to another."

Mark and Helen Carson had no explanation for the odd happenings in their home.

Since the Carson house was less than eight years old, the normal aging and settling processes should have been fairly standardized. They could not be blamed for the strange recurring noises. Nor was there any construction work going on in the neighborhood. The only child in the house was a tiny baby who could not have moved the objects about the residence.

Since no natural answers to the mystery seemed available, Helen Carson decided to take a different tack. She bought a ouija board. Her husband, Mark, decided to have nothing to do with the idea. So Helen asked a close friend, Leslie Martin, to help. Mark Carson, disgusted with the whole thing, settled down to read his paper and the two ladies got to work.

While Helen and Leslie sat without touching the planchette of the ouija board, the ghost or whatever-it-was spelled out that his name was Ralph Gunther.

Mrs. Carson called across to tell her husband what was going on and urged him to join them as the message developed. He reluctantly came over to watch.

The spirit was most explicit.

"I was murdered, here in this house in 1967. The man who killed me was dark-haired and we were in the basement at the time. I don't know what his name was but I'm sure it was 1967. I'm not going to tell you why he did it."

Then the ghost addressed himself to Mrs. Carson. He tried to convince her that she should go and look behind the furnace where he claimed the incident had occurred.

Helen was reluctant but bravely started for the basement stairs. The lights went out as soon as she entered the hallway. Frightened and confused, she quickly returned to the living room.

The ghost reiterated his order.

"Go and look behind the furnace." Ralph spelled out on the board, "Go alone!"

On the advice of her husband, Helen refused to go. She asked the spirit why she should have to go alone.

The angered spirit spelled out the single word, "Gone."

The communication session was thereby abruptly ended for the evening.

Local reporters tried to find out who Ralph Gunther was. A check of police records for that particular period showed no murders, unusual deaths or even missing persons reports for anyone of that name. It is possible that Mr. Gunther was visiting Scarborough and was a stranger in the area where he was killed. But, it does seem odd that no one missed him sufficiently to notify the police. Or was he perhaps involved in some illicit enterprise?

Reporters and television crews investigated the basement, paying particular attention to the area behind the furnace. There was nothing to be seen.

At any rate, the mystery remains unsolved. According to Mrs. Carson, there was a previous tenant, a Spaniard (dark hair ?) who did indeed vacate the house in 1967. Apparently the police would like a few words with this individual on another unrelated matter, but they have no evidence to link him with the murder of one Ralph Gunther.

Helen Carson was not afraid of her ghost ; she wanted to help him. He even cleared the table for her sometimes, making this the first incident I encountered in which a ghost assisted with the housework.

Helen had to reprimand Ralph like a child because he kept stealing and hiding her cosmetics. They seemed to fascinate the light-fingered spirit. The missing articles were usually returned to the exact spot from which they were first taken. Sometimes they were gone for as long as a month.

The one serious problem with this otherwise inoffensive resident ghost was in connection with the Carson's baby. The child, reacting instinctively, became quite hysterical when the invisible being was anywhere near. Mrs. Carson had to order Ralph to leave the baby alone.

An uneasy truce existed the last time I spoke to Helen Carson. Ralph was leaving the baby alone, but the family had decided to move away. They were most anxious to forget about Ralph and this futile search for an unidentified killer. Helen Carson had had enough of ouija boards and unsolved mysteries.

THE HAUNTED STAIRCASE

Toronto's Old City Hall, a Victorian structure in midtown, has caused many arguments in its time. Is it worth preserving? Is it a beautiful example of Victorian architecture, or is it a horror? It is certainly old enough and intricate enough in design to encourage ghosts. So it wasn't surprising that Old City Hall started yet another controversy when it produced a ghost on one of the back stairways.

As witnesses, we have two Judges who held court in the building. And you can't ask for much better witnesses than that.

Provincial Judge S. Tupper Bigelow was the first to notice the strange footsteps. The year was 1965.

"My office was located on the second floor. I began using the staircase which is a convenient way to go downstairs to our common room. On more than one occasion, I have heard these footsteps. I couldn't see anything, but I could feel my robes being plucked. There was no chance that the robes might have caught on anything as I walked downstairs."

Judge Peter Wilch also used the staircase. He, too, heard the mysterious footsteps. On one occasion he heard them ahead of him on the stairs. It is difficult to imagine a dignified judge chasing up a flight of stairs after an unseen intruder. But that is exactly what Judge Wilch did. Following the sounds he went right to the top floor. He began a careful search of the entire area. The place was empty. There was no one there.

Had the invisible being turned around and passed Judge Wilch silently on the staircase, or was it standing there at that very moment watching his reaction to the empty room? The judge came to no conclusion.

Judge Bigelow is reported to have said,

"I'm an agnostic on the matter of ghosts, but how do you explain something like that?"

The footsteps heard in this case are light, suggesting a woman or a child. They appear to be confined to the staircase and there seems to be no harm intended by the haunting. The activities of this spirit have, to date, been restricted to the plucking of passing judicial robes.

No one knows where the ghost, if that is what it is, comes from. There is no record of a murder or even an accidental death having taken place on the staircase of Old City Hall. Could it be that a civil servant actually enjoyed her job in life so much that she is still returning to it after death? And, if this is true, is she also fulfilling a life-long urge to tug at judges' robes?

George Thompson is a member of the Old City Hall maintenance staff. He denies the suggestion that there are any ghosts lying in wait on the stairways. According to Mr. Thompson, anyone who heeds such a story should be considered " daft".

HISTORICAL GHOSTS

William Lyon Mackenzie is perhaps Toronto's best-known historical haunt. But Toronto's very first ghost is likely that of William Jarvis, founder of a powerful and wealthy family when Toronto was York, the capital of Upper Canada.

Jarvis street, known across Canada as a place of dubious reputation, is named after William's eldest son, Samuel Peters Jarvis. The family's first house, built in 1795, was located at the corner of Duke and Sherbourne Streets. It was considered to be a fine, large establishment. And it was in this house that William allegedly came back, much to the discomfort of the new owners.

The house had been sold as a chop house 'and billiard room. From 1832 to 1837, it was owned by a James Kidd who evidently ran it as an inn. During the night, strange noises came from the room once used by William Jarvis as an office.

The groans and noises in that bedroom were so violent that eventually people refused to sleep in it. But it is reported that a visitor from England, by the name of Baxter spent part of one night there. He could not stick it out and fled sometime in the small hours of the morning declaring,

"Never again! Never again!"

The owner, James Kidd, was convinced that the house was haunted. He made a habit of creeping about in the middle of the night, pistol in one hand and a lamp in the other to catch the ghost. However, he didn't succeed. The room was left empty after Baxter's flight and it was assumed that William Jarvis had been the ghost that alarmed him.

Jarvis seems to have come back to haunt his house shortly after his death. William Lyon Mackenzie, Toronto's famous rebel and first mayor, waited one hundred years before making things uncomfortable at 82 Bond Street.

Mackenzie House is situated in downtown Toronto. In Mackenzie's day it was known as York. The homestead is now a popular tourist attraction run by The William Lyon Mackenzie Homestead Foundation. This is a nonprofit group operating the house in trust as a historic site and shrine.

Mackenzie himself, a scrappy little Scot, was long a thorn in the side of York's powerful ruling establishment. He founded a newspaper, The Colonial Advocate, which constantly attacked the government. In 1828 he was elected to the Legislative Assembly of Upper Canada and in 1834 he became the first mayor of the city of York.

The old printing press which figures in the tales of the Mackenzie hauntings, was bought by the fiery William in the year 1825. Although it looks quaint and a bit fragile, it is in working condition according to the label. It is kept locked, however, so that it is impossible to turn the handle and make it run.

The house, located on what is now a building-packed street, consists of two basement rooms, two rooms on the main floor, two bedrooms on the second floor, and a flat on the top, or attic level. At the time of the reported hauntings the printing press was situated in a basement room. The piano, also a feature, was located in the main floor parlor.

William Lyon Mackenzie died in this house in 1861. Since no reports about his ghost appeared until 1960 it can be assumed that he was in no great hurry to get back. He died in a great deal of physical pain and much mental anguish and heartbreaking bitterness. One might take from this that the ingredients of a ghost story are indeed present.

The Mackenzie hauntings were reported at some length in the Toronto newspapers. The believers and the non-believers had a field day. Two caretaking couples swore out affidavits about the spirits they had seen. There were subsequent denials from one of the couples. An exorcism service was held. And finally, the story died down and became legend.

Here is a report on the happenings from the beginning to the last faint echo.

"We hadn't been here long when I heard the footsteps going up the stairs. I called to my husband. He wasn't there. There was no one else in the house. But I heard feet on the stairs." — Mrs. Alex Dobban, wife of the caretaker of Mackenzie House, June, 1960.

"From the first day my husband and I went to stay at Mackenzie House we could hear footsteps on the stairs when there was nobody in the house. Nearly every day there were footsteps at times when there was nobody there to make them." — Mrs. Charles Edmunds, wife of the caretaker of Mackenzie House from August, 1956 to April, 1960.

"You knew you weren't alone." — Mrs. Winnifred McCleary, caretaker, November, 1966.

The story first broke in the Toronto Telegram when Mr. and Mrs. Alex Dobban had been caretakers in the house for a little over a month. They had arrived in April and in June they were so disturbed by the happenings that they handed in their notice. It was to their advantage to stay in the position and so their sworn testimony carries some weight.

Mr. Dobban was retired on a pension from a maintenance job in a downtown Toronto office building. The comfortable though small flat at Mackenzie House was free and there was a small salary that went with the caretaking job. Alex Dobban considered the whole thing a good arrangement.

But in June the Dobbans packed their bags and moved out of the flat to a rented apartment elsewhere. They stayed on the job until a replacement could be found. When he resigned, Alex Dobban had no other job in sight.

"We couldn't stay any longer because of the effect this place was having on my wife's nerves. The things she heard were getting her down. We wouldn't have left otherwise but she couldn't stand to stay overnight."

That was Mr. Dobban's statement when they left. The disturbances were not confined to footsteps. Mrs. Dobban said that one night she woke up to hear a rumbling in the basement. At first she took it to be the oil burner but when her husband checked the furnace wasn't on. The noise she heard, Mrs. Dobban thought, was the locked printing press running in the cellar.

PIANO IN THE NIGHT

On another night she clearly heard the piano playing in the parlor. The Dobbans were in bed, the house was locked up for the night, and there was nobody else in the building.

"It wasn't a tune," Mrs. Dobban said at the time, "It was just as if someone was hitting the keys with closed fists or a child playing the piano."

When asked if she believed in ghosts Mrs. Dobban said she didn't know how else to explain the happenings.

The Toronto Telegram tackled this interesting bit of ghostlore with enthusiasm, sending veteran reporter Andrew MacFarlane to find out what lay at the bottom of the mystery. He found that the previous caretaking couple had experienced even more weird events than the Dobbans. They had left, too, but had been reluctant to tell their story at the time.

Now Mr. and Mrs. Charles Edmunds said that they had stuck it out for three years and in that time Mrs. Edmunds had lost forty pounds. It was the constant strain, she said, of knowing there was somebody else, invisible, in the house.

"One night I woke up about midnight though I am normally a good sleeper," Mrs. Edmunds recounted to the Telegram reporter, "I saw a lady standing over my bed. She wasn't at the side but the head, leaning over me. There is no room for anyone to stand where she was. The bed is pushed against the wall. She was hanging down like a shadow but I could see her clearly. Something seemed to touch me on the shoulder to wake me up. She had long hair hanging down in front of her shoulders. Not black or gray or white, but dark brown. She had a long narrow face."

About a year after this event, Mrs. Edmunds saw the lady again. This time the ghost reached out and hit her in the eye. When she woke up her left eye was purple and bloodshot. To complicate things even more, Mrs. Edmunds sometimes saw a small, bald man in a frock coat in the second floor bedrooms. (Pictures of Mackenzie show him wearing a red shock of hair, but it was a wig. He was completely bald, the result of a fever). Mrs. Edmunds saw both these figures on eight or nine occasions.

There are other witnesses to the haunting. The Edmunds' son, Robert and his wife sometimes stayed overnight with their two small children. And each one of the group had some kind of tale to tell. Robert heard the piano playing in the night and along with his father, went down to the parlor to investigate. They found nothing.

A PECULIAR PLACE

The children were frightened by a lady in the bathroom. Susan was four at the time and Ronnie three. They had gone down to the secondfloor bathroom during a visit, and their grandmother found them huddled on the floor. Their screams had brought her to investigate. The children said a lady had been in the bathroom but had disappeared.

To add to the confusion, somebody or something watered all the plants one night and left mud on the curtains. The house was locked. The Edmunds found no explanation for this weird event and so they finally decided to leave the job, although it suited them in every other respect.

In his sworn affidavit, given to the Toronto Telegram, Edmunds states,

"Certain happenings during the three years and eight months we lived there have convinced me there is something peculiar about the place."

The Telegram published two stories about the haunting, one on June 27 and one on June 28. The Toronto Daily Star, not even waiting for the second instalment, pounced on the ghost story with a stern debunking on June 28.

The whole ghost business was a put on, said the Star solemnly, a dream from the over-heated imagination of a publicity writer. The Foundation wanted to draw attention to Mackenzie House as a tourist attraction and this was their way of doing it.

According to the Star, Alex Dobban 'huffily denied

originating the tales of the ghostly doings' and further-more Mr. Dobban said there was 'nothing to it'. The fact that he had moved out of the free apartment had nothing to do with ghosts, the Star alleged.

Mr. Dobban failed to explain in the Star's story why he had consented to swear out an affidavit if he knew his story was a lie. No mention was made of the Edmunds or their version of the haunting.

By June 30 The Telegram had received a deluge of letters and telephone calls about supernatural experiences. Everybody had a ghost story to tell. One caller reported that there was the spirit of a murderer tramping the steps of Gibraltar Point Light over on the Island. Another story emerged about a Rosedale ghost who actually killed a youth in a ravine mausoleum because the boy had dared to invade the family crypt. This tale was one hundred years old.

Another caller said that he once visited a haunted house, no location given, where he saw a loaded tea tray rise from a table, hover there for an instant, and then settle down without breaking a cup.

None of these stories added anything to the Macken-zie House Mystery but they showed that people were interested in ghosts.

SEANCE ?

Meanwhile, the Star was not idle. While the Telegram published a report on its readers reactions, the Star organized a seance. In retrospect, this ploy sounds even odder than the alleged scheme of the publicity writer who started the whole thing in the first place.

In the light of what happened that night, it is a pity the Star did not keep the seance a secret. Somehow, the word got out and property damage and mob confusion followed.

Seven spiritualists gathered together around the Mackenzie dining room table. The large oil painting of William Lyon Mackenzie looked down upon them. The seven (one of them a newsman) placed their hands palm-down upon the oak table and waited for Mackenzie or one of his relatives to appear.

Although bodies vibrated and there was a weird series of Morse code rappings, one of the spiritualists dismissed the action as unimportant.

"That's nothing," he said, "After all, with seven spiritualists in a room you're bound to get some reaction."

Mackenzie didn't appear. Harold Hilton, one of the mediums present said,

"This definitely proves that Mackenzie House isn't haunted. After all if William Lyon Mackenzie was coming back he would certainly communicate with those who understand him."

To anybody who has read much about spirit manifestations, Mr. Hilton does not sound as if he would understand much about Mackenzie's problems. No ghost is compelled to show up at a given time or place just because seven spiritualists happen to gather together. There is no literature to support Mr. Hilton's stand that Mackenzie's failure to appear on that particular occasion means he 'definitely' isn't in the house.

Aside from Mackenzie's possible lack of interest in the seven spiritualists, there is another reason why no sensible ghost would have shown up that night.

According to the Star, dozens of youths and girls roamed the grounds during the seance, yelling, laughing, shining lights in windows, jumping over hedges and opening doors. Police were called to break up a mob session at midnight. The rear door was forced open and a fire extinguisher was emptied into the hallway. A cement bird-bath was smashed and flower pots broken.

"This is a house of calm," said Mr. Hilton, ignoring the noise and destruction outside. "A place of great tranquillity. There are no spirit influences here."

Being a little more cautious, but still firmly on the side of the debunkers, Reverend W. C. Partridge of Springdale Spiritualist Shcurch, one of the sitters, told the press :

"We're sensitive people and there are always some spirit bodies present but we are sure there is no evil spirit or ghost at the Mackenzie Homestead."

There seems to be a little disagreement between the two gentlemen about whether there were or were not spirit bodies present. They did agree, though, that Mackenzie hadn't appeared.

An appeal was made to the clergy of Toronto to assist with an exorcism service. Exorcism is defined as the expulsion of malign spirits from an object, person or habitation by ritual means.

EXORCISM

Archdeacon John Frank of Holy Trinity Anglican Church responded to the call. On July 2, accompanied by a reporter and representatives of the Homestead Foundation, the Archdeacon toured the house praying in each room. In his prayers he asked that the disturbing spirits leave the Homestead forever. He also asked God to visit the house and drive from it all torment, unhappiness and fear. He prayed for Mackenzie and added another prayer that "this house may long stand as a monument to those who pioneered in this country."

For several years nothing more was heard about ghostly activity in Mackenzie House. Caretakers came in by the day and the flat was closed off. People who requested it were refused permission to remain in the house overnight.

Then in 1962 while some renovations were going on in the house, another report came out about unexplained activity. This time it came from the workmen who, eleven in number, went in each morning and left each night locking up the house behind them.

The foreman, Pat Ryan, reported that things were moved in the night.

"Dropsheets over the old printing press were pulled back," Ryan said, "And a sawhorse and a rope were moved."

The house was locked and there was no sign of a break-in. On one occasion, though, the house was broken into and an electric saw taken.

Murdo MacDonald, a workman, came in one morning to find a hangman's noose over the stairway. He didn't know how it got there. He couldn't tie a hangman's noose himself, he said, nor did he know who could.

Another workman said he wouldn't spend the night in the house if somebody paid him. Nobody offered, so he didn't have to consider the prospect.

Silence fell again, at least as far as the working press was concerned but in November of 1966 a new caretaker, Mrs. Winnifred McCleary, thought the place was still haunted. The toilet flushed by itself and the hot water tap was often turned on.

"You knew you weren't alone."

Striking an entirely new note, Mrs. McCleary said the ghost seemed to put its arms around her sometimes. Mrs. McCleary did not sleep in the apartment, though, having her living quarters elsewhere.

Since that time, some six years ago, there have been no new reports about ghostly activity in the Mackenzie House. Possibly it is all over. Authorities on supernatural manifestations say that eventually a ghost will disappear through lack of energy, if nothing else.

Perhaps Mackenzie grew tired, or perhaps he was satisfied that he had drawn attention to the house and to himself. Possibly, more reports will show up in the future.

The last report, that of Mrs. McCleary, which mentions turning on taps and the flushing of a toilet is reminiscent of a haunt which evidently lived in the house of a Canadian couple in London, England.

The Brandons moved to London in 1966 where they bought a town house in the middle of London. It was a new house, but obviously built on a site where older houses had once stood.

Clair Brandon was an executive, and his wife Inez had once been a model. They had three small children and a dog. Neither of them had ever been involved with ghosts, nor had they thought about it.

On New Year's Eve, 1968, all the Brandons except two-year-old Anna, were in the living room. They heard footsteps on the stairs, and thinking Anna must have climbed out of bed and was coming down in the semi-darkness, Inez went to help her. There was nobody on the stairs. Inez went upstairs and found Anna sound asleep in bed. Obviously she had not been out of bed, nor on the stairs. All members of the family heard the steps.

The ghost inherited by the Brandons liked to play tricks. A favorite was to turn on the water taps in the bathroom. A young woman, sitting the house and dog for the weekend and quite alone in the house, was astonished to suddenly hear the bath water running. When she went to investigate, the tub was filling up. She could find no way to explain it.

Nobody ever saw this spirit, and the house was so new that it was thought the ghost must have come along with the property. This has been reported many times, and in a city as old as London, the ghost could have been connected with something far back in the past. Perhaps it was fascinated with the modern water system.

SEARCH FOR GERTRUD

Sometimes a ghost-hunter sets out to track down information about a specific ghost, only to discover a totally different spirit in exactly the same location. That is what happened during the search for ghost Gertrud.

I first heard about Gertrud through *Weekend Magazine* writer Doyle Klyn. In a column published in 1972, Mrs. Klyn described Gertrud as being "a splendid apparition who suitably haunted an old house in Brockville."

Mrs. Klyn stayed for a while in the Brockville house. She heard all about Gertrud, and became familiar with some of the spirit's antics.

"If Gertrud was feeling haunty, she'd trip you up on the stairs, or blow open doors on a calm night, or sob her way along the upstairs hall. One day a small boy and a large dog stared for three hours at a corner of the ceiling in a room Gertrud was obviously haunting."

It all sounded fascinating, but it took a bit of research to discover just how interesting this particular spirit really was. For Gertrud was a composite of two different periods.

In 1900, the Brockville house became a part of St. Alban's School, a private boarding school for boys. The headmaster of the school occupied the house with his family.

The top floor of the residence was a full-size attic used only for storage. The second floor rooms were bedrooms, four of which faced the front and were, by our standards, large. The house had fourteen rooms in all, with old fashioned twelve foot ceilings and a large fireplace (still usable) in almost every room.

During the late nineteen-thirties, peculiar things began to happen in the big house. No one seemed to be able to explain them.

One of the St. Alban's schoolmasters was noted for his

exceptionally brilliant mind which, when under the stimulus of alcohol, "would be inspired to extraordinary flights of imagination". This man could not endure the mystery. And apparently it was he, in an alcoholic and euphoric state, who invented Gertrud. He left the final "e" off the spirit's name so as to be more suitable to those Hitlerian days. From that time on, the nonexistent Gertrud was given the credit or blame for any strange happenings in the house.

Gertrud was therefore, a creation of somebody's imagination, merely a bit of decorative trimming.

But, despite Gertrud's failure to measure up, things kept happening. There were other reports, much like that of Mrs. Klyn. They all dealt with an unhappy incorporate woman in the upstairs area of the old Brockville house. Gertrud may not have been present, but something or someone was obviously using the site when conditions were suitable.

A woman, dressed in period clothes, was seen retreating along the upstairs hallway when, in fact, no one else was anywhere near the area.

Early one morning, a woman sleeping upstairs awakened to see a female wearing old-fashioned clothing, sitting on a chair beside the bed. The groggy human, unperturbed by the intruder, murmured a sleepy "Hello" to the silent figure and went right back to sleep.

Another incident, also involving an unidentified woman, occurred to an elderly domestic employed in the house in the early nineteen-forties. She appeared at breakfast one morning looking somewhat concerned and inquired who had been crying during the night.

The school director's family was puzzled. None of them had experienced any difficulty during the previous night. But the domestic insisted that she had been awakened in the middle of the night by the sound of a woman in great distress. She stood the crying as long as she could but, when the weeping continued unabated, she got up, opened her door and looked out into the dimly lit hallway.

There was no one to be seen, and the crying ceased.

One has to go back into the past to find anything that might account for the weeping spirit.

The old Brockville house was built by Benjamin Chaffey. He named it "Somerset House" after the English county from which the Chaffey family had emigrated following the War of 1812. Chaffey was a master of engineering design who is credited with the planning of the Victoria Bridge in Montreal and the Morrisburg Canal, among others. He lived in the house with his wife, Janet, until his death in 1867.

Janet Chaffey was present when her husband died in one of the front upstairs bedrooms. Apparently she was extremely upset at the time. One can imagine her going down the hall in tears. It is fairly certain that the sobbing upstairs ghost encountered by Mrs. Klyn and others should have been named "Janet".

The imaginary ghost Gertrud has, over the years, become superimposed onto the real story of the Chaffey family.

Ignoring the fictional Gertrud, we are left with the seemingly logical assumption that Janet Chaffey's ghost has periodically reenacted the occasion of her husband's death. This is not an unusual sort of thing, but it can be upsetting to those who encounter it unprepared.

There have been no recent reports of either Gertrud or Janet, but this case does illustrate how fact and fiction become blended with the passage of years. There is also a fair chance that Janet Chaffey's spirit is somewhere in the neighborhood. She seems drawn to the old Brockville house.

St. Alban's School closed in 1948, and a riding school is now situated on the fifteen acre estate. The house is little changed since the Chaffeys lived there. The verandah was removed to allow more light into the rooms and the small front porch is now enclosed. The original shutters are still stored in the cellar. But whether 'Janet' will ever walk in the corridor again remains to be seen.

THE LITTLE STREETSVILLE SPOOK

Some ghosts have incredible staying power. They are able to remain on a single site for many years — longer than the average human lifetime — without indicating any reason or purpose for their faithfulness. One such spirit is that of a young girl, about seven years of age, who has continually made her presence felt since the turn of the century.

Just outside of Streetsville, Ontario, there stands an enormous old place, the age of which has been estimated at a minimum of one hundred and fifty years. This house sits on a three-acre site near the junction of Mississauga Road and Steeles Avenue, and its extreme age and size make it an almost classic spot for a prolonged haunting.

Over the years, almost every resident of the large house has come to realize — some quickly and others more gradually — that there is something wrong or unnatural about the inside of the building. Some of them have even been able to see the little girl spirit. She is dressed in an old-fashioned high-necked nightdress and is usually observed on the stairs. This child seems to be included whenever the house is sold, an exciting and unspecified part of the standard sales agreement.

The house has four bedrooms, two of them large, one small and one very low with a crawl space. There is a very large farm kitchen with meat hooks hanging from the ceiling. The living room is unusually spacious and the beamed dining room has an open fireplace. All the ceilings are high and most of the floors are made of pine.

A creek running through the Streetsville property forms a large pond behind the house in the spring and early summer.

A doctor and his wife were the first to discuss the little ghost with the press. They found living in the house a most enjoyable experience and considered it a happy home filled with peace and warmth. Their young children played for hours near the supposedly haunted area. During his residence in the house, the doctor was a bit concerned that his children might fall down the stairs. He closed off the stairway and may have instigated the later banging which led people to believe the ghost was once trapped on the stairs.

The next family to move in also had small children. They reported odd things happening but were still very happy with their home. The husband, investigating a strange rattling noise, encountered the little girl.

"There she was, standing on the stairs, in a night-gown. Her hair was blond and she seemed to be clutching at a toy. We figured the room at the top of the stairs had once been a playroom because our children spent so many happy afternoons there."

Those who cannot see the little spirit are still aware of her presence. Doors are rattled, as if by a human hand, throughout the large house, and the one installed by the doctor by the steep stairs seems to receive special attention. Most of the spirit's activities are restricted to the area in and around the stairs, indicating the child was most familiar with that location.

The woman who told me about this inoffensive little ghost lived in the Streetsville house for a period of eighteen months ending in 1972. She never saw the child personally, but ran a constant battle with the lights along the stairway. If she turned the lights off, they would suddenly go on again and, if she wished them to be left on, the chances were fairly good that they would be turned off. Someone or something was playing tricks.

The electrical peculiarities had nothing to do with the basic wiring in the house — lights went on and off at apparent random in the basement and upstairs despite checks by several disbelieving electricians.

There were no children in the house at the time of the trouble with the lighting and the most frequent rattling and banging incidents. Those who were familiar with the house suggested that the increase in activity might indicate that the small spirit was bored because she had no one with whom to play.

The atmosphere in the Streetsville house is not particularly frightening unless you are the sort of person who becomes nervous in any old building. There has been nothing malevolent about the little girl or her actions to date. But, like any child, she does get bored and likes to tease.

Animals in this house have reacted strongly to the unseen presence. One dog, in particular, was very upset. He would rush towards the stairs suddenly, only to slink back into the living room fearfully with his tail tucked between his legs.

In February of 1972, this house and its resident spirit provided an excellent example of how different people react to their first contact with elements of the supernatural. A young girl, in her early teens, was visiting the people who owned the house. She had no knowledge of the history of the building but, after only a very short stay, suddenly announced that she was leaving and would never return. She refused to discuss the reason for this decision — and left.

So, perhaps the spirit of this little girl appears friendly only to those who are prepared to accept evidence of the truly unusual without emotional turmoil. She seems to love having children about the house.

INDIAN LAND

Since this is a book about Canadian ghosts, it is only natural and fitting that at least one Indian spectre should be included. Ironically, this modern story shows once again the marked tendency of the white man to force the Indians from their own land. In this case, the Indians involved registered their objections in a most unusual way.

In the spring of 1972 in the town of Mississauga, two young boys, one eleven and the other thirteen, went to their mother with a problem. They claimed that they were unable to fall asleep at night. According to the boys, a bright light shone into their bedroom and it seemed to come from the far corner of their back yard.

The skeptical parents investigated. To their surprise, they discovered that the boys were, indeed, telling the truth. There was a strange, seemingly sourceless, light in that corner.

The father explained to his sons that he thought rotting stumps might be the cause of the light in the yard. The matter was, for the time being, forgotten.

Shortly after this incident, the two boys ran screaming with fear to their parents. An Indian man was looking in the window at them.

The boys insisted their story was true. No amount of parental coaxing could overcome their refusal to sleep in the bedroom overlooking the backyard. Their mother decided that she needed help in dealing with this unprecedented situation. A friend urged her to contact a local woman who is a medium and a psychic.

The psychic, intrigued by the story, arrived the next morning. In broad daylight, she was able to 'see' what had frightened the two boys. There, in the middle of the backyard, stood a tall Indian male. His face was painted, and he was wearing only a loin cloth and a simple head-dress.

The psychic did some research into previous uses of the land. She discovered that the back yard of the boys' house just touched upon the edge of a burial ground once used by the Mississauga Indians. From that information, it was surmised that the lone Indian might have been a witch doctor or chieftain defending, even after death, the hallowed ground threatened by the encroaching house.

Using a crystal ball and automatic writing, two useful tools in the correct hands, the psychic was able to convince the Indian to leave. She assured him that no harm was meant to his ancestors and convinced him that he could honorably end his long period on guard duty.

The boys were able to return to their room. No further incidents were reported.

Several days later the psychic received another request for help. This time, she found herself in the same neighborhood, but there was an important difference. The house to which she had been called on this occasion did not just touch the edge of the Indian burial ground. It had been built so that more than half of its area was within the boundaries of the cemetery.

Entering this second house, the psychic instantly felt a heavy pressure on her chest. It was difficult to breathe. The unhappy people living there were constantly plagued by what several doctors had dismissed as psychosomatic illnesses.

The wife was afraid that she might be losing her mind and her marriage was on the verge of collapse. Everyone who entered the house experienced sudden blasts of cold air, ill health and fits of bad temper.

The once-beautiful hardwood floors were water-spotted and the whole atmosphere was very depressing.

The psychic was unable to deal successfully with this situation. She admitted as much, a sign of a true psychic as compared with those who will never confess to weakness or lack of ability. A witch was called in to assist and, together, the two women were able to manage the removal of the spirits from the house.

The witch used ancient rites of witchcraft for this truly difficult and complicated exorcism. She refused to discuss her methods in any detail.

At least four Indian spirits were living in the troubled

house. There were men and women as well as a small child that kept crying. Naturally enough, they were reluctant to leave the burial ground; they felt the area was their own. It took several long nights to convince this group from the past that they ought to leave.

Since that time, the resident family has been in perfect health. The blasts of cold air have gone, and the floors are actually responding to special treatment. Domestic relations have improved tremendously and everyone involved is hopeful that the last of the Mississauga Indians are finally resting in peace. Since many houses touch upon this grave site, it is quite possible that other cases involving Indian spirits will occur as time goes on.

I asked the psychic who was involved in this experience to explain how the Mississauga Indians were capable of understanding her communications in English. She explained her belief that a learning period of sorts takes place after death. During this interval, which varies in length, long dead spirits teach the newly dead the various methods of communication with the world of the living. This would constitute a kind of parallel to the English School for Mediums. This theory would also explain why there is frequently a delay between the time of a person's death and that individual's first appearance to us as a ghost.

THE RETURN OF TRAVERS ALLAN

Sudden and violent death sometimes acts as a catalyst. Apparently it allows certain spirits to return to important locations from their past life. Just as the spirit of Tom Thomson sometimes returns to the area he loved above all others, so another man's ghost came back at least once to a favorite spot after his death.

In 1880, Alex Allan and his wife, Eva, purchased a large waterfront property of forest and water located about three miles from Brockville. This property, known for many years thereafter as "Allan's Point", was one of the most beautiful sites on the whole St. Lawrence. It possessed an unsurpassed view upriver to the island-lined horizon and the meeting of water and sky.

The Allans had a son, Travers, who was fortunate enough to spend all his summers from earliest childhood on his parents' wilderness property. He loved its tranquil, unspoiled beauty of woods, rock and river.

Alex and Eva Allan spent every summer at Allan's Point. They built a cottage, "The Shanty", overlooking the water.

In 1911, Eva Allan, by this time a widow, sold the lakefront property and the small cottage that had been erected there. This action must have been a blow to Travers, but he was working in a Montreal bank at the time and Mrs. Allan did not wish to remain alone in a cottage filled with memories of her husband.

In 1923, Travers Allan embarked on a trip around the world, during the course of which he visited Egypt.

Children who had known Travers were given a rather moralistic story about what happened to him in Egypt. They were told that he was repeatedly warned not to venture out alone to admire the beauty of the pyramids by moonlight. The story told how Travers disregarded the warning and wandered out by himself. His punishment for failing to heed the advice of those more experienced than himself in such matters was to be set upon by Arabs who robbed and murdered him.

The adult version of Travers Allan's death is quite different. It is probably more accurate. Apparently a bullet from the gun of a jealous husband had ended an affair as well as the life of the not-so-young philanderer from Brockville.

Regardless of which version one accepts, one thing is fairly certain. Travers Allan died violently and suddenly while in Egypt.

In 1931, the Mainwaring family of Brockville had the

use of the property originally purchased by the Allans. Along with their young children they were enjoying the beautiful scenery and solitude in much the same way as Travers Allan had done before them.

One hot sultry summer morning, eight years after the murder of Travers, Mrs. A.G.M. Mainwaring decided she had had enough of Brockville. She wanted to get away completely from the heat and housekeeping. She decided to seek a cool refuge amid the peace and quiet of Allan's Point. And, since Mr. Mainwaring was golfing at the time, she decided to go alone.

Mrs. Mainwaring jumped into the car. Then she noticed the family's little dog, Brownie, looking beseechingly up at her from the front steps, begging to be taken along on the excursion. Wishing to be completely alone, her first reaction was to say "No" but, unable to resist the appeal in his eyes, she relented and opened the back door of the car. The joyful Brownie was up on the back seat in an instant.

Arriving at her destination, Mrs. Mainwaring moved a light chaise out onto the rock in front of the cottage which still commands such a wide vista of water, sky and distant green islands. She spent a gloriously relaxed afternoon, along with her delighted dog.

When dusk came she glanced to her right, towards a rock which sloped down to the water's edge. It was fifteen or twenty yards from where she was sitting. To her surprise, Mrs. Mainwaring saw a man.

The stranger was sitting quietly, gazing silently up the river now bathed in the late afternoon glow of approaching sunset. He had not been there a few minutes before; nor had there been any indication of human presence the entire afternoon.

Startled at the intrusion, Mrs. Mainwaring stared at the man. Brownie, who had been lying contentedly on the ground beside her, now saw the stranger and reacted instantly. He jumped to his feet, growling softly in the back of his throat. The hackles rose on his back.

Before Mrs. Mainwaring could decide to move or speak, the figure melted into the rock before her astonished eyes. The man was gone without a trace.

"Come on, old girl", said Mrs. Mainwaring to herself. "It's time we went home!" Gathering up her things, she called the dog and the two of them departed with despatch.

Some time later, Mrs. Mainwaring told her close friends, Judge and Mrs. Edmund Reynolds, about the encounter. The Reynolds, long-time Brockville residents, had known the Allan family well. When Mrs. Mainswaring finished describing in detail the appearance of the apparition, the Reynolds looked at one another, and almost together said,

"That was Travers Allan!"

Chapter Nine

GHOSTS ON GUARD

POWER OF THOUGHT

Research into the historical background of a haunted house may reveal that one or more of the former owners or occupants was morbidly interested in certain aspects of the supernatural. Past owners may have vowed — not merely to return and visit their earthly home, but to remain there indefinitely and deliberately drive off any newcomers. Living in such a house may prove to be impossible, even physically dangerous, for the persons who unknowingly acquire the property.

A spirit may refuse to give up its old and prized possessions. It may not even tolerate the occupancy by strangers of a certain room to which it attaches particularly fond memories. Ghosts can be just as materialistic and selfish as any living human.

There seem to be those among the dead who resent any real or imagined indignity to their mortal remains or last wishes. A great many years ago, Sable Island was occupied by an incredibly nasty group of people. They were not merely content to loot the many ships smashed up on their shores by the wind and waves, but set out beacon lights to entice ships onto the rocks and certain destruction. Any survivors who managed to make it to land were immediately robbed. The victims were murdered in order to prevent later identification.

A young woman was among those who fell prey to the Sable Island wreckers. Her spirit is still reported on the island today, identifiable because of the fact that the apparition lacks a ring-finger. The wreckers removed it in order to steal her ring. The woman's ghost searches endlessly for the missing finger, indicating that perhaps there is some basis to the belief that a body must be buried intact in order to find some peace in the grave.

Objections to incomplete burials have been with us for years, an integral part of our folklore. But now they are leading us into new and far more complicated problems as the wishes of the deceased run up against the advances of modern science and medicine.

From Chicago in March of 1971 came a quite astonishing report. It appears that the recipients of transplanted organs are being haunted by the ghosts of the dead donors! The spirits involved seem to be demanding the immediate return of their bodily parts. Dr. Hyman Muslin, assistant professor of psychiatry at the University of Illinois, made the report. He asserted that some patients believe that they are "being attacked by the ghosts of the cadavers, punishing them for the crime of acquiring a kidney."

Since both the transplanting of organs and the extensive study of the effects upon the recipients are relatively new fields, we will have to wait until more research has been completed before reaching any conclusions about this quite unexpected obstacle. Dr. Muslin has been studying kidney transplant patients for more than two years now. He says that their inability to accept the idea of acquiring another person's organ may prove to be a greater threat to their lives than the body's purely physical rejection of the foreign kidney.

One transplant patient in particular was reported to be having quite serious problems. He was firmly convinced that he was being haunted by the "hovering spirit of a man who had died at the age of twenty-eight and whose kidney he had received." Perhaps this man was merely feeling a natural guilt that he was still alive while the young donor of the kidney was dead. Feelings of guilt combined with a vivid imagination could produce the concept of an avenging spirit. But it would not be too surprising to eventually learn that there is some justification to this man's insistent claim that he is being haunted by the youth's angry spirit demanding the return of the acquired kidney.

Ghostly demands that a specific body be buried intact are far from new; it is the ramifications of such requests upon future transplant operations that make the Chicago study so interesting.

Active and violent protest may be launched if a spirit discovers the misappropriation of personal articles. Many people assigned to the sad task of sorting out the intimate belongings of a deceased relative have complained about experiencing a distinct and unnerving feeling that they were being watched. This is not a pleasant sensation, and those who have encountered it will usually back off hastily the next time someone is needed for such a chore.

From the staging of a funeral to the handling of personal belongings, many of us have been guided by the phrase, "My friend would have wanted it that way." This attitude is not a humorous one, because occasionally the person involved will take pains to make sure things are done in a proper and fitting manner.

A cheap or improper funeral can throw a spirit into an absolute frenzy. Even structural renovations have been known to cause quite severe repercussions. Doors will bang shut, china will be flung onto the floor and smashed, and the peace will be completely shattered until someone manages to placate the unhappy instigator of the violent activity.

And it is sometimes difficult to find out just what is causing the spirit's concern. The needs and requests of a ghost are not always rational in our eyes. Like angry children, some ghosts calm down only when they have managed to get their own way. But, unlike dealing with children, one cannot simply apply the rules of Dr. Spock or send a ghost to its room for a cooling-off period.

LEPRECHAUNS

It was in order to avoid just this sort of supernatural temper tantrum that the runways of Shannon International Airport were rerouted in 1958. According to Hans Holzer, the original plans would have led the engineers into a direct conflict with an established settlement of leprechauns or fairy-like creatures. These are not ghosts, of course, but there are certain similarities between the forms.

Many people ridiculed the idea of being dictated to by a group of elusive little men. It was decided, however, that the risk was simply too great to take. The construction workers refused to touch the circular, bush-enclosed fairy meeting place.

The Irish, in general, believe in ghosts and most other manifestations of the supernatural. They are also a practical people when it comes of avoiding unnecessary trouble with the unknown. Possible interference with the landings and take-offs of modern aircraft struck them as being a very serious matter indeed.

Call it silly superstition if you wish. The plans were finally altered to the satisfaction of everybody — with the possible exception of the unfortunate individual who had designed the plans that were rejected.

The active protest of the spirit world against any outside interference is now considered to be one of the primary reasons for burying people on or near the site of hidden treasure or contraband. The spectres involved appear to take a personal responsibility for concealing the secret and they are usually quite successful in discouraging any would-be interlopers or thieves. Most robbers would sooner face a fully-armed night watchman than tangle with the supernatural.

The cruel and sudden termination of a young and innocent life was thought to create the most angry and vengeful of spirits. Because of this ancient belief, children were once slain, deliberately and violently. Their bodies were then placed in the foundations of buildings. In this way, their ghosts were supposed to provide protection for the completed construction.

The remains of such small victims are still being unearthed today, although one hopefully assumes that this wicked practice has completely died out with the passing of the years. While there have been instances of treasure being protected by ghosts, it has never been conclusively shown that buildings receive the same attention from the spirit world. By now, education and social pressures should have resulted in the cessation of some of the more violent and excessive practices linked with legend and superstition.

It was not only children who were murdered in order to provide spirits for the protection of possessions, buildings and buried treasure. Nor are we in any position to sit back smugly and assert that this barbaric sort of behavior only occurred in other, less civilized, countries. Fully grown adults met the same fate right here in Canada. Pirates, smugglers, wreckers and murderers are all a part of our national heritage. We have a colorful and violent past.

Many stories of protective arrangements based upon death come from the Eastern Maritimes, from Nova Scotia and the seaboard in particular. Ghostly figures stand guard to this very day over buried pirate chests. These guardian ghosts, generally former members of the group that concealed the treasure in the first place, spend an indefinite period of time on active duty. It is not known if the discovery of the treasure frees them from their long and lonely assignment. Opinions vary on this matter. Their vigilance has lasted, in some instances, for well over a hundred years.

In the Maritimes provinces, many complicated rules and formulas have evolved from the various attempts to outwit and rob the spectral sentries. This challenge should not be underrated. Hidden treasure still lies undisturbed along the coast, but it usually takes a brave and somewhat desperate individual to try to wrest it from the sand and guardian ghosts.

Silence, timing and respect are believed to be three ingredients essential to a successful treasure-hunting expedition. Courage is another requisite and the hunter should be quick of mind and fleet of foot. If a digger is provoked into speech, and this often happens, he thereby enables the guardian ghosts to exercise greater power than usual. He may even bring about his own death or serious injury during the ensuing chase. The treasure could also vanish back into the wet sand forever — a sad ending to dreams of discovering a mighty fortune.

Superstition holds that guardian ghosts cannot cross water. Difficult to believe as this may seem, it has become accepted as fact over the years. It shows a total disregard for basic logic that a landsman should be safe from the spirits of former sailors when he has managed to place a body of water, however small, between himself and any pursuers. For this rather peculiar reason, flight across a stream or into a small waiting boat are considered to be among the best methods of escape in case of difficulties.

Oak Island, off the North Shore of Nova Scotia, has been the site of many a treasure hunt. History has it that Blackbeard's treasure lies buried there. Contending with ghostly figures and the strange reverberating sounds of shovels involved in ancient burials unnerved most of the original treasure-hunters. The old belief that the search should be conducted after dark never did add to the peace of mind of those involved. This concept was soon abandoned in favor of daylight labor when the tides were right.

OAK ISLAND

The Oak Island search has gone on since 1795. Some of the men simply ran out of time, money and energy; others fled in total panic and disillusionment.

Modern knowledge and the addition of heavy excavating equipment have not made searching this area any more successful or enjoyable. The legendary money-pit resists and eludes discovery. No one is even sure what, if anything, lies beneath the many layers of sand and mystery. As Mr. Kerry Ellard of Montreal, the public relations man for one of the groups on the island said,

"It is awfully difficult to say when it will end. We don't know what we are looking for. No one does. There is a terrific body of evidence which indicates there is something there. But just what it is or how it got there we don't know."

Still, the Oak Island challenge is accepted as eagerly today as it was many ago when the first clues were discovered. At last report, in February of 1971, men were renewing the digging once more. Dan Blankenship is a former Miami contractor now charged with supervising the operations of a company called Triton Alliance Limited. This, the latest group of treasure-hunters, is more formidable than its predecessors. It consists primarily of a hardnosed bunch of realistic individuals who are working to the best of their ability with some mighty big money to back their efforts.

The Triton men are planning to utilize the most modern scientific methods in their digging operation. You can also bet that they will be mindful of the fact that six men have died to date in the attempt to solve the Oak Island mystery.

The six deaths on the island were not natural, but there is no reason to believe that they were caused by spirits. I could find no information about the first two fatalities. Four men died in a single incident in 1965. Robert Restall was working in a pit at Smith's Cove when he was overcome by carbon monoxide gas. His son and two workmen tried to save him and all four perished.

A short time ago, there was a newspaper article about Oak Island. In it, Dan Blankenship was quoted as having stated emphatically,

"I have been involved with this damned island, one way or the other, since 1965, and I learned a long time ago that it doesn't pay to look for simple answers. We are now pressing ahead with new equipment, which might bring us final answers to the whole mystery in the next few months."

Mr. Blankenship may be an optimist of the highest calibre. But many people in Nova Scotia and across Canada are hoping that these stubborn men will clean up the entire mess in short order. It is felt that they should find a treasure worthy of their effort and end the reign of superstition and fear on the island.

It would be a shame, however, if this new crew were able to produce explanations for all the weird events that have taken place on or near the job-site. But that would be highly unlikely. I doubt if anyone will ever be able to spoil the reputation of Canada's haunted island.

MARKS OF VIOLENCE

Just as guardian ghosts remain to protect treasure, it seems that powerful thought patterns can permanently influence their surroundings. Violent deeds sometimes leave indelible and recurring impressions, very real imprints, where they take place. For example, grass cannot be grown on certain spots where infamous events occurred in the past. The ground becomes lifeless and unresponsive to seeding. Even common weed spores blown by the wind are unable to sustain life on such a patch of earth.

Similarly, some floors and pieces of furniture have uncanny stains that defy explanation. These markings are usually believed to have been caused by blood spilled in an earlier violent incident. Such stains may appear and then vanish without reason. In this respect, psychic markings have a lot in common with hindsight and other associated phenomena. When a deep impression has been made, through shock, upon the mind of an individual, that person may well return in his original surroundings as an apparition for contemporary viewers. So the stains caused by violence can return.

It is up to the individuals who encounter such odd markings to try to determine their origin. This is a task which is frequently very challenging, involving a total historical analysis of the area.

A young man was convicted of first-degree murder in the Maritimes. Up until the very moment of his hanging, he emphatically protested his complete innocence with respect to the charge. He seemed so utterly sincere that those present for the hanging were much impressed, but they could not alter his sentence.

The man then gave his official executioners specific instructions. They were to watch his grave carefully in the years to come. In return, he promised to provide them with undeniable signs of his innocence.

To this very day, his grave is said to be the best-tended in the entire cemetery. Although it receives no special attention, the grass on that particular plot is always greener and more luxurious than on any of the others. The drainage, quality of grass seed and general care are the same for each plot; the result is not.

It would appear that an individual with enough strength of purpose can, indeed, accomplish strange things even after physical death. This ties in neatly with the many stories of spirits who return in order to fulfill vows made prior to their death. The common ingredient seems to be the simple determination to prove a point. Motivation appears to be the all-important factor in many of the supernatural phenomena. The power of the human mind should never be underestimated; a thought can protect a treasure, scar a plot of land, mark furniture or promote unusual growth. It is worth considering that perhaps death actually frees people to accomplish things they couldn't do in life.

Chapter Ten

GHOSTS OF THE NORTH

THE STRANGE GUIDE

Near Whitehorse, a man was saved from possible injury and serious trouble through the timely intervention of a ghost from somewhere in Canada's past history. He was in his mid-thirties, a Korean veteran, and not at all a highly imaginative or nervous individual. I will refer to him simply as "Jerry" throughout the story; he prefers it that way.

In the fall of 1970, Jerry set out with his dog on one of his frequent prospecting trips. He entered the desolate country near a place called Pelly Crossing. This is located above Whitehorse and inland along the Mayo Dawson Road. It is an isolated area.

As Jerry wandered through the scrub brush, he became engulfed in what is locally called 'muskeg". Water and certain mosses accumulate in hollows in the surface of the land to form this unpleasant, frequently treacherous, bog. It is difficult to walk in.

Every step Jerry took led him farther into this seemingly endless muck. He was determined to go on but there appeared to be no way in which he could proceed without becoming even further entrapped. Even retracing his steps seemed impossible. Being unfamiliar with the area, he believed that in order to get out of the mess he had no alternative but to plow stubbornly ahead through all that muskeg.

Eventually Jerry came to a small elevated area where there was just enough wood to prepare a small fire. By this time, it was growing quite dark so he wisely decided to spend the night on the hillock in relative comfort and security. The problem of finding his way out could wait until morning.

Jerry lit his fire, and collected some wood to keep it going. After preparing a small meal, he wandered over to sit under the only tree on his small island. Being tired and discouraged after his travels that day, he sat quietly with his head resting on his knees.

Suddenly Jerry's dog became very agitated. It snuggled in as close to its master's legs as it could. Jerry lifted his head to see what could possibly be frightening his usually calm animal. In front of him stood four men and a girl who looked about seventeen. And all of them were ghosts!

"I can't explain how I knew they were ghosts," said Jerry. "I just knew they were, and so did the dog."

One of the men began to speak to Jerry in a tongue utterly unknown to him. To his utter amasement, then and now, he found that he understood perfectly what was being said.

"There they were, all five of them, in the middle of nowhere. And they weren't Indians. They all had white skins and looked like they might be Anglo-Saxon. But the language certainly wasn't English or French. I'd have recognized either of those languages."

One ghost appeared to be leader of the quintet. He began to shout at Jerry for being on that particular spot. He was apparently simply furious at what he believed to be a deliberate intrusion and challenge. Jerry, after war experience in Korea, was quick to respond. He jumped to his feet without really thinking about his next move and started after the offensive spirit. All five ghosts then disappeared.

Jerry and his dog settled down again, thoroughly confused but still convinced that the incident was over. A short time later, the dog began to get upset and worried again. Jerry raised his head once more and there they were. The same five beings were standing staring at him.

The spokesman, the same as before, began to shout with rage. But this time the girl seemed to be disturbed by all the commotion. She even tried to intervene on Jerry's behalf as the quarrel became increasingly violent in tone.

Jerry rose slowly and deliberately to his feet. And, on this occasion, he resorted to some rather abusive language in his demands that these creatures go away and leave him alone. They vanished into the night.

For the third time, the exhausted prospector settled down with his head on his knees. And, just as before, the dog began to shiver and whimper with fear. When Jerry looked up this time, however, he saw only the girl standing there. He spoke to her in English, and she answered him in that strange language he could not identify. Despite this difference, there appeared to be no language barrier. He was able to understand her exact meaning without difficulty.

The girl ghost said that she realized Jerry was lost. She

then proceeded to give him explicit instructions about how to get out of the muskeg in the morning. Then she disappeared.

Jerry saw none of the ghosts again, although his night in the wilderness was far from restful.

Early the next morning, Jerry packed up his few belongings and got ready to leave. Remembering the girl's directions, he decided to gamble that the whole thing hadn't been a figment of his imagination. He took the route she had suggested. He came upon each of the stones and landmarks that he had been told to watch for along the way. Soon he was free of the muskeg.

So far, nobody has been able to identify the five ghosts or even classify them in general terms. One possible source may be the scattering of Europeans who filtered through Canada and the United States in the 1880's. Encountering ghosts at any time is still considered unusual; to deal directly with white spirits speaking a foreign language in that isolated part of the country is unique.

ESSPIE

Cats are generally supposed to have a special place in the world of the supernatural. But Esspie is one cat who doesn't have the least bit of rapport with spirits. Certainly nobody could say that she had any influence over their activities. In fact, Esspie seems to be the victim of a group of particularly sadistic ghosts. They seem to consider her to be some sort of fascinating furry plaything.

It began early in 1961 when Esspie was acquired by the Ingersoll family. The Ingersolls had built their house on a rather unusual site. It stands on top of an ancient Indian battlefield close to the Alaska Highway in the Yukon. It is because of the site and its bloody history that the ghosts who attack Esspie are assumed to be dead Indian warriors.

"These ghosts kick our cat without warning, sending her a good three feet into the air," Mrs. Ingersoll says, "Other times she will be sleeping quietly in the rocking chair and all of a sudden she will be pushed out of it with one swipe. Esspie has been kicked by these invisible things so many times that there are days when she can't be forced to go near a pair of boots."

Even though this cat was named 'Esspie' because of her repeated encounters with the supernatural, it hasn't helped her much. Humans in the house are left alone but the cat is not. The attacks come without warning and last for only seconds.

"There just isn't time to contact the spirits and try to pacify them." Mrs. Ingersoll says, "Besides, we have no idea why they go after Esspie."

It is hoped that Esspie can survive these mindless attacks. One wonders if she can see her tormentors, since animals are said to have powers beyond ours. Perhaps Esspie knowns exactly what they look like, these strange creatures who insist upon using her as an unwilling football.

SIMON FRANCIS

Even those who possess an innate psychic ability and strong mental control can encounter unexpected trouble when they resort to the use of the ouija board in a quest for detailed information. One highly qualified and experienced individual in northwestern Canada can and does testify to this point. This woman has studied supernatural manifestations for many years and frequently serves as a consultant for others doing research in this field. On the theory that experts know best, I will relate the incident in her own words as much as possible. The name of the ghost has been changed to provide some minor concealment for the identities of other individuals who were involved.

The plane crash in the following story was covered by the press. The incident is real.

The sequence of events got under way in the mid nineteen-sixties.

"This was in the days when I would, if asked, fool around with the ouija board. At this time there was an American pilot, by the name of 'Simon Francis', who was attempting to fly, non-stop, with a small plane from Alaska to the southern United States. He didn't make it and crashed somewhere north of Whitehorse. The wreckage wasn't found until almost a year later.

Everyone who could was aiding in the search. Since we were living in the area then, we were very interested in what was happening. So, one night, a couple of ladies from the airport came over. They knew I had played around with the board before and asked me to try it again with them. The idea was to see if we could locate the pilot, if he was dead as they thought. Nutty me, I agreed!

Thereby began such a series of events, it finished me on the board for good. We got him loud and clear! He tried so hard to tell us where he had crashed, and every time it proved wrong.

He first told us he had crashed near Canyon City, so in all earnestness we phoned the searching party of fliers in Whitehorse and told them what we had found. We also told them how we had done it. They were skeptical, as well you can imagine, but nevertheless they did search it out. But no sign of him was found there.

Then we realized that, being an American, Simon really didn't know much at all about Canada. Later we got the bright idea of using an Alaska-Canada aerial map and then we hit pay dirt! We put the little planchette down on this and Simon went right to the place where he was later found.

We didn't report this finding as we felt we had dug enough into it. The man's buddies were there for the search, but they were too skeptical to try the 'medium bit', so there was no chance to hold a session to prove our findings for them. They took off, back to Alaska. We figured if they weren't sufficiently interested, then we weren't either."

(If you think this woman is being cold-hearted, reconsider for a moment. It had already been established that Simon was dead. Finding the plane at this stage was of only academic interest — It was too late to help the pilot in any physical way. Since the man's friends were prepared to accept his loss, it would have been futile to make them remain in the Yukon. It would also have been quite out of character. Those who have genuine psychic ability are most reluctant to force their views upon others who do not understand.)

But the story doesn't end with the return of Simon's friends to their home in Alaska. Simon had been summoned through the ouija board and he had come.

"Then we found that we couldn't get rid of him. Talk about teleportation! Things would disappear like magic around the house, and I could always feel it when he was bugging me.

One day I was all alone in the house and was preparing to go to the store. So I laid ten dollars on the dresser and went to the kitchen for something. When I came back, in a couple of moments, my money was gone! No sign of it. Out loud, I said, 'Simon, I know you're there. Put that money back.' No dice.

A few days later, I was sewing at my machine and I needed some black elastic. I called to my older daughter to bring me some from her kit. She did, and placed it right on the machine in front of me. Then I dropped my needle and just bent down for a fraction of a second. When I sat up again, the elastic was gone. Again I repeated my orders — to no avail. He was always doing things like that ! He always made quite sure we knew he was in the house !

Through the board, Simon told us all about himself, his family, his girl friend's name, all about his father. All this proved to be true, as we were able to check these things out with his friends."

At first, Simon seemed like an amusing and childlike visitor to the members of this Yukon family. Indeed, he could not have picked a more tolerant and understanding group upon which to practice his pranks and talents.

But ghosts are a bit like fish — after a while, they start to go bad. Simon began to exceed his welcome and the limits of good taste. He interfered with important family matters, and became a general nuisance around the house.

Simon proved to be quite capable of petty jealousy and, as he realized that the family were tiring of him, put up a stiff fight to be allowed to stay.

"He admitted to taking the money and the elastic and many other things, but wouldn't tell us where they were. Instead he would just write, 'Ha ! Ha !' across the board. He said he did it just for kicks and that we'd better get used to it."

Then began the period of seriously trying to get rid of Simon. This family attempted all sorts of things to force or persuade the spirit to leave. They tried various exorcism rites and ordered him to clear out. But Simon liked it there; he enjoyed the attention given to his activities and resisted strongly. These people had their light-fingered ghost living with them, complete with increasingly nasty little tricks, until 1970. At that time, a highly skilled medium was able to oust the stubborn ghost.

Keep the story of Simon Francis in mind whenever

you are tempted by one of those innocent-looking ouija boards. It is sometimes easier to make contact with the supernatural world then it is to break off ensuing communications. In fact, the open sale of these boards can get innocent people involved in matters far beyond their comprehension and control. The maunfacturers of ouija boards claim that they are selling only simple imaginative games, but a great deal depends upon the personalities of the individuals using the equipment.

A boy in his late teens told me that he had contacted the devil during a session, his first and last, with a ouija board. He may have only imagined the incident, but the important thing is that he really believed that the communication took place. The experience thoroughly frightened him.

In general, a ouija board is a very poor choice of gifts for a sensitive young person and should be handled with care even by those possessing some skill in dealing with the occult.

THE CAT IN THE STORM

It couldn't have happened, but it did. Readers of science fiction are familiar with the theory that spirits transfer into new bodies after death, and that the new bodies need not necessarily be the same shape or type as the old one. This story adds an additional twist to that theory, and it is not the work of a science fiction writer. It really did happen as reported.

Near Haliburton, Ontario, there is a winding road that twists, turns and rambles its way through the thickly overgrown bush country. Only four houses have been built on this road so far. The houses are not situated close together as one might expect; they are separated by distances varying from one to one and a half miles.

Mr. and Mrs. Barry Neilson (not their real name) are an older, retired couple who live in one of these isolated houses with little contact with the outside world. They did, however, have a much beloved dog. The animal was their only companion in a very lonely existence. It had a special bed, and always received extra bits of meat after the conclusion of the evening meal.

In the early summer of 1965 the dog died, leaving the two old people even lonelier than before. They hesitated about getting another animal. Both of them felt that nothing could replace their former pet and fill the emptiness his departure had caused in their lives. Besides, they simply didn't feel up to going through the training program all over again with a new puppy.

Winter came and, with it, a mighty sleet storm that lasted for more than twenty-four hours.

Just before supper, the Neilsons were interrupted by the familiar sound of loud scratching at the front door. It sounded very much like the noise their dog used to make when it was anxious to get in the house in a hurry.

But, when they opened the door, the animal standing there covered with sleet was not a dog. It was a large grey cat.

The startled pair let the cat in, and carefully towelled the wetness from its fur. They had no idea now it had managed to find the house. All the access roads were closed due to the severity of the storm, and the nearest neighbor's house was more than a mile away.

The cat went right to where the dog's bowl had once stood. It was an unusual spot in the corner of the dining room, but the cat went directly there instead of into the warm kitchen where the food was being prepared.

After feeding the strange animal, Mr. and Mrs. Neilson ate their own evening meal. They took their time, lingering over the coffee, only to be interrupted by the cat's activities.

The animal went into the kitchen and scratched on the wall beside the sink. This was an exact repetition of the actions frequently taken by the family dog when the Neilsons had tarried too long before fixing his special after-dinner treats. The scratch marks were still visible on the wall.

Then Mrs. Neilson had an idea. She went towards the kitchen and stood quietly by the door. In a low and deliberately even voice, she began to go through a list of different names. There was no response from the cat until she reached the fifth name.

As soon as Mrs. Neilson uttered a certain word, the animal stopped its scratching by the sink. It walked over to her and rubbed up against her leg. The cat had answered to the dog's name !

The astonished pair were not given much time to recover from their surprise. Directly after finishing off the last of the table scraps, the cat went to a cupboard in the entrance hall. It stood there as if waiting for them to make the next move.

For a few long minutes, the Neilsons remained motionless. They just stood there and stared at the cat. Both were remembering that their dog had once slept in his padded bed just inside the cupboard door. The door had been left open in those days to allow him freedom of access. The bed was still there in the cupboard, although no one had been near it since the summer.

Finally, Barry Neilson went to the cupboard. Meeting his wife's frightened eyes, he slowly opened the door. Without hesitation, the cat walked right in! It turned around a few times and then settled down to sleep in the dog's bed.

After puzzling over the cat's behavior, the Neilsons finally locked up the house and got ready for bed. But, first, they both peeked into the cupboard. The cat was still sleeping peacefully, as if it hadn't a care in the world.

The next morning, the cat was gone. A careful room-to-room search failed to uncover anything, and the elderly couple could not discover how the animal had left the house. None of the neighbors had lost a cat, and nobody was able to account for the strange appearance of the animal that stormy night.

When asked for their reaction to this peculiar experience, the Neilsons replied that they were surprised and a little frightened. But, on thinking it over afterwards and discussing the matter in some detail, their general reaction had been one of pleasure. At their advanced stage of life, they took some consolation in interpreting the events as an indication of an existence after death.

THE TRAP LINE GHOST

The following example is not really a contemporary one. It took place in the winter of 1933-34. It represents an almost classic example of the supernatural and shows what can be accomplished after death. It is also the first time this story has been given to a writer for use.

Because this experience took place in the western sector of our country, it is unique. It used to be believed that all such occurrences were somehow restricted geographically to the eastern Maritime provinces. Enough cases have come to light to prove that this isn't the case at all.

Gordon Sculthorpe was about twenty-five at the time of his one and only encounter with the supernatural. He was trapping north of Fort St. John in British Columbia. Even today, there are great stretches of isolated country up in that area.

The main village in the district was formed by three trading outposts, the main post being the one operated by the Hudson's Bay Company. Around the three posts were the various groups of Indians, some of them Cree, but mostly Beaver Indians. From there, the trap lines ran outwards in all directions.

It was a life few city dwellers can understand. Even before the snow came, all the travelling was done by pack pony or saddle pony. When the men were going out to their trap lines, they would put packs of up to thirty pounds on pack dogs. In the deep winter, the freight supplies were hauled in to the posts with horse-drawn sleighs.

Mr. Sculthorpe says that his trap line was not one of the better ones. It started fifty miles from the outposts. There were five cabins located along the line, each about 9 feet by 12 feet, with logs up to 4 feet high and a sod roof.

The interiors of the cabins were dug down to about 3 feet, and the dirt was used for the roof and to bank the outside walls. The spaces between the logs were chinked with moss and mud.

Each cabin had a cache, a small storehouse built up on the top of poles. The poles had stove pipe tacked around them so that animals could not climb up to get at the supplies and furs kept there.

One cabin was a few feet larger than the others and this was the one used by Mr. Sculthorpe as a "home cabin." The others served as overnight stops along the trap line.

The cabins were about fifteen miles apart and the trapper usually managed to arrive at one each night. Sometimes, however, he spent the night with only spruce boughs as protection against the temperatures of thirty or forty below zero.

It is almost unnecessary to point out that Mr. Sculthorpe was in a place where he didn't receive any mail for the entire winter. What happened to him was a simple enough incident, or so it seems on first glance.

Mr. Sculthorpe tells about the experience he has never forgotten.

"At that time, I had three brothers, one sister, mother, father and my mother's mother in the family.

One night in January, while I was sleeping in the home cabin, something woke me up. I was really awake because I got up onto my elbow. And there was my grandmother standing in the doorway! I asked 'What is the matter?' She smiled, and then slowly faded away.

' When I got back to civilization (the outposts), it was already April. There was a letter waiting for me, informing me that my grandmother had died that night in January."

By our standards, this man seems rather young to face an entire winter of total isolation, but that was how he made his living and he had accepted the conditions as did many others during that period of economic depression. He did miss human contact and the letters from his family that would have informed him about events in the outside world.

This is one incident that is hard to blame upon prior knowledge of a forthcoming event. The young man did not even know that his grandmother was ill, and he was certainly not expecting her to die on a specific date. He was totally isolated from any outside sources of information, and had to rely upon the evidence of his own senses. The fact that the woman died the very night he saw the apparition in his cabin is impossible to label coincidence.

Some interesting questions about ghosts arise out of this experience. It is natural for the spirit to have wanted to reassure her absent grandchild after she died, but how was she able to find him? How could she have travelled that far in such a short space of time? She was literally in two places at once. Given the choice of five equally isolated cabins, this ghost went directly to the one in which her grandson had elected to spend the night.

Chapter Eleven

SEEING THE FUTURE

THE WOMAN WHO WEPT

Forerunners, foresight and double-vision are serious terms that can be used to indicate supernatural warnings or indications of approaching events. These events may be either good or bad. Traditionally they are connected with impending death and deep personal tragedy.

Death in a house may be signified in advance by a bird beating against the windows or becoming trapped within the building. The whirring sound of invisible wings can sometimes be heard at night long after ordinary birds have returned to their nesting places.

Disaster is also supposed to follow shortly after a mirror or picture has fallen from the wall. Another version of this belief is that a broken mirror will cause seven years of bad luck.

The music of an organ, choir or violin may be heard several times preceeding the actual event it heralds. But three short distinct knocks at the front door are considered to be the classic form of warning or summons.

Many reports about early Canadian forerunners were collected by Dr. Helen Creighton in *Bluenose Ghosts*. Most of her tales came from people of Celtic descent so it appears that such legendary previews have their source somewhere in Irish and Scottish folklore.

The Halifax area was, and still is, rich with stories about foresight and forerunners. And all across Canada, one can find people who firmly believe in one or all of the superstitions connected with these phenomena.

Such beliefs are, by their very nature, self-perpetuating. They are handed from generation to generation, and seldom challenged. This chain of faith is incredibly difficult to break. If a family member does die shortly after a picture has fallen from the wall, the old belief is reinforced, confirming it once again for all involved. When death does not occur immediately, the incident is forgotten, conveniently but not deliberately, until a later date.

With this sort of highly selective remembering going on, it is hard to separate an actual chain of events from mere coincidence. And perhaps a differentiation should be made between what is accidental, perhaps natural, and the truly unusual. Pictures fall down all the time due to natural causes, but those three knocks on the door can be unnerving.

Forerunners come in many forms. Sometimes they merely involve a sudden inexplicable mood change. One woman in Country Harbour, Nova Scotia, related an experience which could illustrate this phenomenon. It does show that unusual things continue to happen up to the present period and are very real to those involved.

This incident took place in the early nineteen-sixties. The woman was bringing in her washing at dusk one evening when she was suddenly struck by an almost unbearable feeling of loneliness and desolation. There seemed to be no reason for this profound reaction but she began to weep uncontrollably. Something was wrong — but she couldn't think of any explanation for her weird behavior.

Early the next morning, this woman had a real reason for feeling miserable. She learned that two of her best friends had died tragically. The time of the accident matched exactly with that of her attack of unhappiness. You can, of course, argue that this was just an odd coincidence, but it happens frequently enough to warrant attention.

Some supernatural warnings are general; others are quite specific about the identity of those to be involved in the forthcoming event.

A forerunner may be in the form of a noise or mood change. In this respect, it varies from foresight which naturally enough involves a visual experience. Foresight occurs most commonly among those of Scottish or Germanic descent. They seem particularly receptive to advance sightings.

A man who is already dead may appear before his startled wife or keep an important prearranged meeting with a close friend. This indicates that there is a short time allotted for last minute communications.

In many cases, a single person observes the visit connected with a case of foresight. This presents a problem. Not too many people want to talk about such experiences because the story's acceptance depends upon their individual credibility. They don't want to be put on the spot about something they themselves find hard to accept. Then, too some of the visits are of a highly personal nature. This is not so much the case with forerunners which can occur in several different places at the same time.

Foresighted visions may be of a funeral for someone who has not yet died. Some people have accurately reported the preview of a family visit not even in the planning stages when they knew about it.

The first car was seen by those with foresight long before it arrived in their isolated communities. They had no idea what sort of thing was passing them on the road and were frequently terrified by the strange sight ! Phantom trains, cars and carriages were seen and identified well in advance of their actual appearance on the scene.

This particular phenomenon has far-reaching implications. It causes one to wonder just how much self-determination we have over the events in our daily lives. Do we base our actions on rational decisions or are we all moving in a previously determined pattern ? Certainly it would be disconcerting to have someone inform you that your funeral will shortly be passing along a certain road to the local cemetery.

What is even more unnerving is that all human attempts to prevent the fulfillment of foresight and forerunners have failed. Somehow, no matter how hard one struggles, circumstances always combine to prove the accuracy of the prediction. A cortege trying to find a different route may find that the road has been flooded and the major bridges washed away. It will be forced back onto the track indicated in the earlier vision.

Many people claim to possess foresight or what they usually refer to mistakenly as 'extrasensory perception.' Instead of talking about ESP, il would be more accurate to utilize "higher sensory perception." Such understanding is not beyond our sensual abilities; it is simply an area which we have yet to develop to its greatest level.

In most cases, there is a way to check out somebody's ability to apply foresight. Have the individual write down a memo the next time anything odd happens. They should include a detailed description of what has occurred and what they interpret it to mean when applied to the immediate future. Then have the person tell a second individual, preferably yourself, and turn the dated memo over to be checked later.

If the predicted sequence of events takes place, with no outside interference from either of you, the foresight may indeed be genuine. These are very hard terms to fill since such experiences may occur only once or twice in a person's lifetime.

Only recently has man been able to work with extrasensory perception as a definable and measurable entity. In December of 1971, the results of studies at the Maimonides Medical Centre were released to the public.

Contrary to expectation, especially among the female contingent, the Maimonides tests showed that men were better telepathic receivers than women. Emotional messages were more likely to be received than unemotional ones, and distance had absolutely no effect upon the ability to receive. It was also shown that the prediction of the future could be demonstrated in a laboratory setting. In other words, dreams really are the key to the future; we can learn from them.

The Maimonides tests also indicated that mood played an important part in the ability to receive messages. The best subjects were generally those who were very happy and confident, or very unhappy, insecure and dejected. These test results make it easier to understand the unusual mood swings associated with cases of foresight.

The scientists concluded that there was a "definite correlation between mood and the individual's ability to perform extrasensory perception stunts in laboratories." Self-confidence was very important, thereby reinforcing the old belief that many things can be done if only we have sufficient faith in our own abilities.

Just as dreams can foretell the future on occasion, so

the Irish Banshee, or wailing fairy, is considered a fore-runner. It has seldom been heard in Canada, but is still considered synonymous with impending death for those who do hear it. Somewhere along the way, we have created a Canadian substitute for the Banshee. The Demon Dog, or Hell-beast, has a definite place in our early history and legends. It, too, is considered fatal to those who see it or hear it howling.

The Demon Dog may be disappearing with progress, because it has been quite a while since there were any reliable reports about a sighting of it. I could find nobody who had encountered it.

THE CLOCK TURNS BACK

Hindsight is much the same as looking back into time. People have described it as the same as watching a motion picture set with care and an eye for accuracy in a previous period. It generally involves the passive observation of a real event that occurred some time before on the same spot or locale.

The astonished viewer may be utterly ignorant of the historical significance of his sighting — the rare opportunity to watch history in the making, to see things as they really were long ago. No text book could be so accurate.

The people involved in the actual presentation or manifestation act as though the modern intruder were quite invisible to them. They are not affected in any way by the alien presence in their midst. Their actions are completely natural.

This phenomenon has been likened to travelling back-wards through both time and space. The result can be a distinct feeling of disorientation and mental confusion.

One of the most celebrated incidents of what we call h   o women suddenly found themselves in the time and setting of Versailles just prior to the fall of the French monarchy. Buildings were in their original positions and structural condition.

Recovering from their initial shock, the two ladies who were both well-educated wandered about at will. Together, they watched the total reenactment of a peaceful garden scene from many years before.

The ladies were not noticed by any of the individuals that they encountered or observed, despite the fact that their modern clothing would have seemed outlandish when judged by the standards of that particular period. It was as though they had become invisible. No other explanation is acceptable. Had they been visible, their presence in the royal gardens would have provoked a definite reaction.

From this it can be seen that some of the supernatural phenomena can work in two opposite directions. They can bring the past into the present, in the form of a ghost that may be seen by some individuals and felt by others. Or, they can carry particles or representatives of the present back into the past in cases of hindsight. It is really a two-way operation. The main difference is that those involved in hindsight have little or no impact upon their temporary surroundings. They can only watch in wonder. A ghost, on the other hand, can thoroughly upset present existence.

It would, therefore, appear that the past is fixed. It cannot be altered by any actions on our part. Our present existence is still fluid and subject to the whims of such things as spirits from the past.

Many fictional works are based upon the theory that an individual can go back into space and time in order to alter and correct historical events. While this is a fascinating concept, it is not supported by existing research into the supernatural.

Many incidents of hindsight are to be found in the Nova Scotia and Newfoundland seaboard areas. Perhaps this concentration is partially due to the numerous adventures that took place there during the days of the earliest sailing ships.

Boats of all sorts appear unexpectedly. Some sport ancient rigging, and are manned by the shades of sailors in old-fashioned dress. Once-dangerous pirates still row stealthily ashore to bury their bloody treasure. And, late at night, ships that were once wrecked upon the treacherous reefs and rocks repeat their accidents in graphic detail for contemporary observers.

Hindsight viewings recall the legendary tales of shipboard fires that brought disaster to men and cargo alike. Long forgotten ships sail soundlessly across the open harbor, leaving behind them amazing trails of ghostly flame.

Ghosts from the past and viewings into history become intermingled. Sometimes it is difficult to decide whether the past has come to us or we have been temporarily moved backwards.

YOUNG TEAZER

The *Young Teazer* was a privateer operating along the Nova Scotia coast. One day the ship, out on one of its dangerous junkets, was surrounded by armed warships in Mahone Bay. Rather than subject themselves to capture by the British, some of the crew decided to destroy their own vessel and, with it, all evidence of their past illegal activities. The *Young Teazer* went to the bottom of the bay in a fiery blaze of crackling timber.

This all took place in 1813. Under normal circumstances that should have been the end of the affair. But the same ship is still being reported, afloat and ablaze, more than one hundred years after the actual sinking. She was last seen by reputable witnesses in 1935.

The sighting of the *Young Teazer* is more complicated than it may seem at first glance. Some people see the ship and others, on the same spot, are unable to do so. This divergence of opinion may arise from the fact that some people are simply more receptive than others. It could also be the result of a limited few being involved in a brief and exciting hindsight experience. We cannot tell for sure if the sighting is an actual viewing of the original sinking of the ship, or more like a television rerun in which the ship repeats its actions for modern watchers.

Not all cases of hindsight involve the repetition of historical shipping events. Oddly-costumed individuals from all walks of ordinary life have been encountered. Frequently the setting for such meetings is isolated so that, once again, we cannot tell who has travelled in which direction.

Every past generation is represented. Some of the individuals drive vintage cars. These vehicles have been seen as they were repeating road accidents that are on record as having taken place many years before.

It may be that any incident that makes a great impression upon the minds of one or more of the persons involved is somehow indelibly engraved into its surroundings. Given the proper circumstances, and we still do not know what these are, the event can happen again and again, an instant replay of life. The same or similar circumstances can also allow us to visit the past for a short time. A quiet walk in the Canadian Maritime provinces can lead right back into the colorful pageants of history. We have yet to learn how to instigate, control and terminate such experiences.

Chapter Twelve

MARITIME GHOSTS

THE HAIRPIN

The Maritime provinces, perhaps more than the rest of the country, are noted for their interest in and acceptance of different aspects of the supernatural. The stories originating in this area have been taken seriously and are well-researched. They are handed down from person to person over the years.

The fiery return of the *Young Teazer,* the Amherst mystery and the tales of guardian ghosts continue to fascinate those interested in psychic phenomena. These and the many other Maritime experiences make excellent examples of the various manifestations. They form an important basis for comparison with incidents from other areas.

Hindsight may occur in a dreamlike form to the very young or unconditioned individual. It would seem as though a relaxed and undefended mind may be more receptive to such experiences than an active, highly analytical one.

A small girl in Nova Scotia awoke early one morning and rushed to tell her parents about a strange "dream" she had experienced the night before. In it, she remembered having seen a very old lady standing just inside her bedroom door.

The child was able to describe the nocturnal visitor to her mother in surprisingly clear detail for such a youngster. She even recalled that the peculiar old woman wore her hair tied in a knot held in place with a very large hairpin. The result of the child's narrative was an accurate and detailed description of her great-grandmother.

But the little girl had never met the woman; nor had she ever seen a picture of the old lady. There had been no family discussions concerning that hairpin which formed such a crucial element in the total description. The older members of the family would have accepted that particular hair arrangement as usual and not bothered to mention it. Such a hairpin would only have caught the attention of someone totally unfamiliar with its existence. The child, never having seen such a thing, would have noticed.

In a concerted effort to find a reasonable explanation for the girl's dream, if it really was a dream, all the family members got out their old pictures. Scrapbooks and photo albums were dusted off and carefully examined. The child recognized her great-grandmother from a photograph as the woman in her dream. But there was not one picture in the entire collection that showed the hairpin!

The little girl may have had a simple visit from the spirit of the old lady, or she might have been involved in an incident of hindsight taking her back to the days when her great-grandmother had occupied that room. The two phenomena appear to be closely related and, on occasion, may even be interconnected. There was no natural explanation for what happened.

There is one important factor about this incident. The child quite naturally assumed that her visitor's appearence belonged in the context of a dream. She was not upset or afraid. The only difference between this experience and an ordinary dream is that the little girl was able to recall the experience in almost perfect detail the next morning.

THE VIOLIN THAT WOULDN'T STOP

Sometimes a forerunner can be so clear and distinct that, upon looking back, people cannot understand how they failed to heed the warning. Then they are struck by the fear that, even if they had comprehended and acted upon the warning, nothing would have prevented the eventual fulfillment of the predicted catastrophe.

During the early nineteen-forties, a most peculiar event took place in an isolated logging camp near Alma in New Brunswick. The camp was near the area which has recently been allocated for a new National Park.

One evening, a group of men gathered about the camp site after work. They exchanged the usual jokes and tall tales and listened to several fiddlers who alternated in providing the entertainment.

Nothing untoward happened until one of the better fiddlers decided to take a break. The man finished the lively tune he was playing and laid the violin down beside him on the ground. The music should have ceased at that point, but it continued!

From the strings of the violin came three clear and

distinct notes — a high note, a low note and another high note. A bright flash lit the faces of the astonished men as they stared at the now-silent violin.

There was no explanation for the trio of notes or for the sudden flash — no natural explanation, at any rate.

The troubled men gradually trooped off to bed. They were mostly simple, uncomplicated loggers and contractors; what had happened was quite beyond their understanding. They were uneasy and suspicious.

The next day began under grey and humid skies. Thunder rumbled menacingly in the distance as the men moved out towards the stands of trees. Some of them later admitted that they were reluctant to go to work that morning.

Just before noon, a bolt of lightning shot from the sky. It struck a tall tree, felling it and the logger astride its upper limbs. The man, one of those present at the strange events the night before, died instantly.

Coincidence? It may well have been, but the men who heard the violin, saw the flash and witnessed the death of their friend within such a short period of time, never forgot the incident. Many of them passed it onto their children and it is still being discussed and debated today. The story comes from the daughter of the man whose violin was utilized in the forerunner.

Fatalities were not all that unusual in the logging camps, but the incident near Alma had a lasting impact.

RIVER OF DEATH

Great significance has often been attributed to dreams. You can buy books that list meanings for every object or incident in a dream. These lists are supposed to enable you to read the messages being sent from your unconscious mind.

Dream messages, however, do not always originate in the dreamer's mind. They can come from another source entirely. Occasionally they are like forerunners, telling of events yet to happen. And, for some people, it is not too unusual for a dream to come true in terms of a real-life situation.

One well-known dream has brought reassurance and comfort to a large number of people who are convinced of its authenticity. It is the sort of thing that one would like to believe could really happen.

A young man in Nova Scotia was very lonely and unhappy after the death of his father. He had no other living relatives and there was nobody to help him through the initial period of shock and grief. The funeral service upset the young man terribly. His thoughts constantly forced him to wonder what really happened after the death of a human being. He found himself quite unable to readjust to everyday life and was seriously in danger of a nervous breakdown.

One night, the father appeared to his son in a "dream." He reassured the youth and said that all was well now because he was with the Lord. The son looked about carefully. He saw that his father was standing on the far bank of a very wide river. He told his father;

"I wish to cross over the river and join you."

But the father smilingly replied that it would be a great many years before the two of them could be together again. He urged the youth to be patient.

The young man awoke the next morning in a much improved frame of mind. He no longer worried about what would happen to him after death.

Perhaps this dream did come true. The son lived to be ninety-two years of age !

GHOST SHIP

Skeptics feel that the incidents involving phantom ships are merely indicative of some very vivid imaginations and an acute awareness of Maritime shipping history. One of the people who would have heartily agreed with that theory is a gentleman called Bert Wood. He had lived all his life in the Maritimes and had frequently joined with those who openly scoffed at the stories of flaming vessels returning from the past. But something happened to change Mr. Wood's mind after all those years.

The Wood family live in Stonehaven, New Brunswick, about twenty miles from Bathurst. The night of September 9, 1969 was an unusually stormy one in that area. Gusts were blowing at speeds of up to twenty-five or forty miles an hour, and the telephone lines were down.

After an uneventful evening in front of the television, Mr. Wood and his son went upstairs to get ready for bed as usual. Mrs. Wood remained downstairs for a few minutes to finish tidying up.

As she worked, Mrs. Wood glanced casually out across the Bay of Chaleur. Startled by what she saw, she quickly called to her husband and son to watch. It looked as if there was a flaming tanker going up the bay.

Hadley Wood, the son who works at Consolidated-Bathurst Limited, was the first to notice anything unusual. He couldn't quite accept what he saw from the window.

"I told Mom it had to be the phantom ship. It was a mass of light from one end to the other. It was lit up too much for a tanker."

Bert Wood described the rest of the evening to some local reporters.

"The lights would flare up like a house burning and within ten minutes or more, all would die down again until you only seemed to see quite bright lights in the stem and stern, but even these were brighter than normal lights. They were sparkling bright, like a star, and much brighter than those we could see along the water line.

"Then suddenly they'd roll up again. There were

big flames like a burning building. The flames would flare a while, and then fade away to the point where the ship almost seemed to disappear. Then, about fifteen minutes later, the flare-up was so brilliant that you could see the whole outline of the stern and bow."

That's quite a description for someone who is supposed to be an unimaginative and realistic individual. You can almost see the nautical apparition through Mr. Wood's astonished eyes.

The Woods had spent a good part of their lives watching boats cross the Bay of Chaleur. They were not the sort of people to be easily impressed. They were completely familiar with the normal running lights of the average vessel, and with the usual speeds maintained by the different types of boats in the area. And there were no strange boats passing through that particular stretch of water on the ninth of September — the recorded traffic was no different from that found on any other evening.

Mr. Wood went on with his unusual story, specifically commenting on the speed of the phantom ship.

"Vessels travel about twelve to fourteen knots an hour at the most around here, but this one was running that many knots in five to ten minutes it seemed. At first the ship was running fast up the bay, just off Stonehaven and next she was off to the left around the Janeville and Clifton area. It was going so fast I figured she couldn't be an ordinary ship. The ship seemed to be no more than a mile away at times, working inshore and out as it dimmed and blazed."

The Wood family watched the ship with awe until after midnight. They woke their twelve-year old daughter, Betty, so that she could watch with them for a while. They thought, perhaps correctly, that such an opportunity might never occur again. The flaming vessel was worth the sacrifice of a little sleep.

Attempts to contact neighbors ended in frustration with the discovery that the storm had brought down the telephone lines throughout the area. The sight of that ship was the experience of a lifetime, and the Woods were unable to share it with their friends.

When Mr. Wood talked with the reporters, he admitted that he wouldn't be laughing anymore when people talk jokingly about what they call "The Phantom Ship of Bay of Chaleur." He has seen it with his own eyes in the presence of witnesses.

Let us assume for a moment that the entire Wood family was mistaken. If so, what were they watching for such a long time that dark night? There were too many lights for it to have been a tanker. And, besides, no ships of any kind were destroyed by fire that evening. A modern vessel would have had no need to tack against the high winds, but this one was described as "working inshore and out" which clearly indicates a tacking action, utilization of prevailing winds for advancement.

That ship had no business being in the Bay of Chaleur area and we are left with the unmistakable feeling that it may have originated somewhere deep in Canadian history. Three questions seem worthy of consideration. Where did it come from, why was it there that night and where did it go?

THE DUNGARVEN WHOOPER

One of the major problems facing lumber camps is the ever-present threat that log jams will form and prevent prompt delivery of the freshly-cut timber. These jams are quite frightening as more and more logs pile up and increase the degree of blockage. Tangled spars jut up into the air for many feet. A serious jam prevents the water from following its natural downstream direction.

Water behind the jam builds up in pressure until the logs burst free in a sudden, explosive flood.

Just this sort of log jam formed on one of the branches of the northwest Miramachi River in New Brunswick. For days the exhausted men struggled to free the entrapped logs, but the pile-up only became increasingly large and dangerous. And, because the logs were already overdue at the mill down-river, this jam also represented a loss of revenue for all those involved.

Early one morning, a logger named Dungarven jumped up and boldly announced that he was going to tackle the problem single-handed. He was quite determined and told the other men to stand back and watch his skill in manipulating the log prod or pole.

"I'll break that jam or breakfast in Hell!"

Dungarven went out onto the tangled logs while his fellow loggers and lumber-jacks watched in silent horror from the shore. After much hopping about, he managed to release a few key logs and the entire mass began to move. Dungarven let out a triumphant whoop of joy.

The jam broke up with incredible speed as the logs sailed through the air on their way downstream. The breakup was too fast and the water pressure behind the jam too great. There was no time for Dungarven to clamber over to the safety of the shore. He went down-river with the crashing, smashing, newly-freed logs.

Shortly after Dungarven's sudden and violent death, teamsters and lumbermen passing along the logging road beside the Miramachi branch began to report hearing strange whooping noises coming from the river. At first nobody paid much attention to these tales but, with time, a certain constancy of detail began to emerge. Comparison of the various stories indicated that the woodsmen had all heard the same peculiar sound, at almost exactly the same spot. The incidents always occurred at the early morning hour marking the time when Dungarven had died. No one ever heard the whooping late at night or in broad daylight.

Dungarven had accomplished his aim. He had broken up the massive log jam so perhaps he didn't take his breakfast in Hell after all. He or his spirit may still be near the old logging camp, startling passersby.

Each year, during the height of the logging season along the Miramichi, the story of the Dungarven Whooper is told once more. Some people claim that the whooping sound can still be heard at dawn — depending upon the listener and conditions along the river bank.

The strange tale of the Dungarven Whooper varies depending upon the teller and his degree of sobriety at the time of telling, but there does seem to be a factual basis behind it ... faded now after the passage of many years.

This story was first told by Father Williams, a versatile individual who worked as a youth in a Maritime lumbering camp. Later he studied to become a doctor and eventually became a well-known Roman Catholic priest. Father Williams designed and made the Christ the King flag which represents the Vatican internationally.

THE THINGS THAT CAME TO LIFE

The Royal Canadian Mounted Police at Dartmouth, Nova Scotia, apparently have a large, heavy, metal hoop in their possession. It was thrown at two journalists by an angry poltergeist.

The men were investigating a case involving an Eastern Passage family, when the hoop sailed through the air and almost hit them. Apparently the spirit was expressing its objections to their continued interference with its activities. They would have been killed if the thing had scored a direct hit. And there was no reason to believe that it hadn't tried to wipe them out completely.

No one was in sight and there were no markings in the fresh snow that covered the area. What disconcerted the reporters even more was that they were unable to find a single human being who possessed the necessary strength to throw that hoop.

The poltergeistic invasion of the Louis Hilchie family began the day before Christmas in 1943. A board jumped across the room in which the Christmas tree was being decorated.

At first, those present thought a practical joke was being played on them. They changed their minds on Christmas day when an entire cupboard sailed across the room, landed on the stove and then struck the ceiling. Suddenly, it was no longer a joking matter.

The washing machine came loose and skidded up and down on the kitchen floor. Cupboard doors opened and closed, and eggs and butter flew into a mixing bowl as if in preparation for whipping up a cake. Some of these activities led the reporters to believe they might be dealing with a "female" poltergeist.

For days on end, weird but basically harmless incidents occurred in the Hilchie residence. Then there was a change of pace and things began to get really rough. Five-year old Bobbie Hilchie barely escaped decapitation when a heavy hammer flew at him.

The Royal Canadian Mounted Police were called in to help. The Hilchies had never heard of psychic investigators ; they turned to the only source of aid they could think of at the time. The policemen watched with horror as a large bucket of lard, which should have been upstairs, almost struck two of the little Hilchie girls who were playing on the living room floor.

During this period, a man called Earl Beatty was the Maritime manager for United Press. He and another writer assigned to the case were the targets in the hoop-throwing incident which marked the welcome end of this manifestation.

THE BOOTS THAT WALKED

It was just a typical old farm house, one of five such buildings that formed a loose settlement about 3½ miles off the Moncton Highway. The barns were solid and the farm's landholding was close to a hundred acres. The land itself was of excellent farming quality. But, despite these desirable features, the house was deserted. There was evidence of a hurried departure and nobody in the neighborhood was sure why the former owners had left in such a rush.

After the First World War, in early 1919, a returning soldier named Holland moved into the deserted old farm house. He lived alone and, at first, appreciated the peace of life in the countryside.

The quiet was suddenly shattered, however, by the sounds of stamping feet and loud singing voices. Nobody was in the house but it sounded as if an endless party was in progress. Mr. Holland endured the noise for as long as he could. Finally his nerves gave out and he was forced to flee.

Holland went straight to the parish priest and expressed his belief that the farm house was infested by evil spirits. He begged the clergyman to help him regain possession of the house.

The priest accompanied Holland to the farm house and sprinkled holy water about as he blessed the different rooms. He paid special attention to the upstairs area because Holland said that the unexplainable noises seemed to come from there.

Holland moved back into the house. For several days he was left in peace. He thought the trouble was over.

Then, late one night the noises returned, louder than ever. The whole house seemed to reverberate with shouting and coarse laughter. Holland fled to one of the neighboring houses in the little settlement. Shocked at his appearance, the people there convinced him to spend the night with them.

Next morning, Holland appealed once more to the priest for help.

The clergyman did not seem particularly disturbed or surprised at Holland's return. It was almost as though he knew his help was going to be needed. He read through a few books on spiritual exorcism before announcing his decision.

"Alright, this time we'll try something a little different. I'll do more than just bless your house. Instead, I'll try a series of individual exorcisms throughout the house. Hopefully we can manage to drive whatever-it-is into one of the upstairs bedrooms. Don't ever use that room and everything should be okay."

The priest set about his work that same evening. The exorcism rites were read in every room except one of the upstairs bedrooms. In each case, he ordered the offending spirit or spirits to go into the previously selected room. Following the service, the door to that bedroom was boarded shut, never to be reopened.

There was no more trouble with spirits while Holland lived in the house. Some years later, in the early 1930's the house burned to the ground and, since then, nobody has attempted to rebuild on that spot. A neighboring farmer takes care of the land but no one goes near the place at night. The neighbors all refer to the spot as the "haunted Reinsborough Place." The inference is that whatever was shut up in that upstairs bedroom is now at large in the area.

There is another haunted house in the same district. The Fisher Place is about seven or eight miles from the Reinsborough house. The original owner of the Fisher

Place was a very odd character indeed. He dealt in black magic and collected books on satanism.

This strange man wore a tall black hat and sported a full black cape which blew out behind him when he strode about his land. He always carried a carved wooden cane and delighted in terrifying his unfortunate neighbors. He claimed to have the ability to make evil spirits perform at his command and even boasted about using them to fly the year's harvest into the high lofts. Strange carvings adorned the fence posts on his property.

One story in the neighborhood relates that a young man in the area challenged the professed satanist to prove his power. The man in black promptly removed his high boots and set them on the floor. At his command, the boots marched across the floor and then returned to his side. The challenger fled.

When this man died, apparently of natural causes, his collection of books on the occult caused much distress in the neighborhood. Firmly believing that his wicked spirit still resided in the house, people refused to go near the place. For years the building stood deserted and neglected.

In the early nineteen-sixties, an incident took place at the old Fisher Place with tends to support the neighbors' contention. A group of American campers became stranded in a heavy rain storm and entered the old house seeking shelter. These people knew nothing about the history of the house; all they wanted was protection from the elements.

The campers piled most of their gear onto the old trestle table and stacked their light tents in a corner. They prowled about the darkened house wondering why nobody lived there.

As dusk fell, the visitors lit their lamps and prepared to eat before settling down for the night. In the midst of the meal, loud noises echoed through the house. The campers stared in shock at each other. Having previously wandered through the rooms, they knew there were no other human beings in the place. It seemed to them that a heavy-booted person was moving from room to room. But they saw nothing.

Then the furniture began to vibrate violently. The terrified campers left the table and fled into the storm. They never even returned to claim their expensive camping equipment.

The next day, neighbors who had heard about the disturbance came over to investigate. They found the table just as the campers had left it — except that every plate had been turned upside down in what looked like a deliberate action.

SHIP OF FLAMES

This story comes from a natural medium, a woman who has had many strange things happen to her and around her during the past twenty-five years. One of the experiences which made a lasting impression upon her was her first glimpse of a phantom ship on fire.

In 1963, this woman was visiting in a small Maritime town called St. Martin's. This is really more of a village than a town, and is located about twenty-nine miles from St. John in New Brunswick. It is a quiet and relaxing place, and the woman was patiently waiting for the birth of her third child.

Late one fall evening, someone along the edge of the small St. Martin's harbor spotted the flaming ship. From that moment, the word spread quickly. Villagers telephoned each other, and ran to alert neighbors without telephones. From the past performances of the ship, they all knew that they had a minimum of two hours of fun and excitement ahead of them. Sometimes, the ship had been seen for a full four hours.

Attracted by the enthusiasm, the woman joined a group of people standing on a small hill. To her surprise, she could see the burning ship as it moved slowly up the bay just beyond the harbor. It was a masted schooner, something she had never seen before in her life.

The ship moved gradually up the Bay of Fundy and across the harbor mouth. The fascinated observers could see the masts burning and falling as she sailed.

Through binoculars, the view was even better, ending any latent suspicions that one might be watching a large school of herring or something along that line. There was no doubt left in the minds of those who watched from the hill; what they were seeing must have happened many years before.

Gradually, the ship passed from view, her masts now gone, with only the hull on fire in the distance.

Many people saw the ship that night. Obviously it was not necessary to possess any special abilities or powers. There it was for everyone to watch. The villagers said that the same flaming vessel always appeared in the fall, in September or October, if it was going to appear. They freely admitted that there had been some years when they had not seen it at all.

Some people have claimed that this ship is the same vessel that was sighted in the Bay of Chaleur. They may be right, but there is an interesting difference. This boat moves much more slowly, covering the five or six miles during which it is clearly visible from St. Martin's at about two miles an hour.

Chapter Thirteen

BEYOND THE BEYOND

WHO BELIEVES?

Ghosts are becoming respectable. People are willing to accept their existence too easily, just to be in style.

In Canada, despite the absence of numerous authenticated sightings, there exists a strong and growing tendency to accept the supernatural and most of its phenomena.

A test given to a large group of Canadian university students in the early part of the nineteen-sixties found less than ten percent willing to categorically deny the existence of ghosts. Fifty-seven percent of those tested acknowledged the possibility of there being such apparitions in active circulation. The remainder, a large thirty-three percent, expressed a definite belief in ghosts.

This would appear to indicate a surprisingly high percentage of firm believers in this day of skepticism. But, then, ghosts and other related phenomena survived and even flourished in the Age of Reason.

These test results may stem from a need to believe in anything which might be interpreted to indicate the existence of an afterlife. But this sort of desperate grasping at straws is usually associated with older people who realize that they, too, must one day face death. It is odd to find it among students.

There is one disturbing facet about the test results. There was no concrete evidence for the beliefs of those students; they had accepted the supernatural without question, without demanding sufficient proof. Only one of them had ever encountered a ghost; none was able to describe the characteristics usually associated with the average poltergeist. Yet there they were, well over half of them, willing to concede that such astral entities could exist.

Many of the students tested had, at one time or another during their lives, been in a place or situation which seemed very familiar although they had no recollection of such a thing in their actual past histories. They believed that reincarnation was quite possible.

There was another interesting fact about the test results. The survey was conducted in a residential college run by a religious organization but all denominations were represented. There were only a small number of Roman Catholics in the test group.

If, today, the same test was administered to college students or even to high school seniors, I think we would find even more individuals ready to accept all facets of the supernatural too quickly and too easily. The youth of today are highly susceptible to new ideas and messages and, unless warned and guided, they could become the vulnerable targets of unscrupulous leaders and dealers in misinformation.

While keenly aware of the contradictions in their own value systems and those of their parents, young people are frequently unable to see and understand the discrepancies that still exist in the study of the supernatural. The danger is that they may turn to those individuals who profess to have all the answers.

But there are no easy solutions to the many puzzles surrounding the various manifestations. Nobody has all the answers. It is up to all of us to make sure that the youth of today realize this. They must extend their questioning attitude into every field of endeavour. As they challenge politicians, teachers, our sexual standards and the clergy, so they should question evidences of the supernatural.

Right now, perhaps more than ever before, interest in psychic phenomena is on the upswing. We need only to glance at recent television programming to see the reflection of the growing fascination with the unnatural and the unusual. Children watch Sabrina, the Teenaged Witch; House of Frightenstein, Casper and the Groovy Goolies. Teenagers turn to such programs as The Ghost and Mrs. Muir, The Amazing World of Kreskin and Bewitched, while adults scare themselves silly with Night Gallery, U.F.O., Ghost Story and The Sixth Sense. The whole generation is attempting to escape into the world of the imagination and the subject matter is increasingly connected with the supernatural.

Another indication of increased contemporary interest is the fact that psychic bookstores are doing a booming business. Books on the supernatural are selling fantastically well in Canada. A few years ago, it would have been impossible to specialize in this field; now there are several stores featuring psychic literature. So great is the demand that one of our major service station chains offered a small book on basic witchcraft as an enticement to purchase its products. The demand for the little book was great, but so were the clerical complaints. The offer was cancelled.

Following the profitable lead taken by British Overseas Airways Corporation, Pan American Airlines now offers a $629.00 Psychic Tour of Great Britain. This tour does more than just provide entrance to a group of haunted houses. It includes a visit to a psychic healing centre, a seance and a day to be spent at Stonehenge with an important Druid. Even the flight dates are astrologically plotted so as to favor the travellers. What better way to cater to those interested in the supernatural?

What does this increased interest mean? It does not necessarily reflect a healthy attitude. It is especially bad for susceptible individuals who approach such matters mostly on an emotional and uncritical level. Some people can cope easily and intelligently with new and unusual ideas and material; others need guidance just to deal with everyday existence. Thus the increased interest in the supernatural has both positive and negative aspects.

This growing popularity of the occult can be dangerous unless our religious leaders produce some evidence of their own to counterbalance the extreme generalizations being spread by confidencemen and mere opportunists. They need a central clearinghouse of information dealing with matters of the supernatural, an ecumenical place to which people could go to receive advice and the most up-to-date material available.

There is yet another, equally important, reason why we require a qualified central leadership in the field of the supernatural. Along with the growing fascination with the occult by thoughtful intelligent individuals is a macabre searching for some of the less savory aspects of the study by youngsters and those of lesser intelligence. These, in turn, become the victims of old wives' tales, misinformation, lurid movies and publications and imposters who pretend to have the required information at their finger tips.

What kind of trouble can come from indiscriminate delving into all aspects of the supernatural? Unethical leadership is the greatest threat, people who take advantage of innocent curiosity. As Owen Rachleff of New York University puts it.

"Most occult-niks are either frauds of the intellectual and/or financial variety, or disturbed individuals who frequently mistake psychosis for psychic phenomena."

These, the people described by Mr. Rachleff, are the danger. They can capture the imaginations of individuals who lack the intelligence and information to challenge this leadership and demand sufficient evidence before seriously committing themselves. It is the minds of the young and ignorant that are at stake.

THE BLACK ARTS

Religious leaders and genuine psychic investigators alike are dismayed by the increase of interest in the "Black Arts". This field has, quite accurately, been referred to as "Devil Worship."

On May 4, 1972, Dr. Donald Morgenson, a psychologist at Waterloo Lutheran University, addressed a conference of the Ontario Association of Childrens' Aid Societies. He said that the young are turning away from reality towards witchcraft, telepathy, astrology and palmistry. He believed that this was because they had been denied a vital period of childhood innocence. He claimed they "would like to take that fatal step into the past where things were clearly more human, more innocent, more childlike." Dr. Morgenson did not point out that these youngsters may see their parents heading in the same direction.

Even earlier, in November of 1971, a Church of

England spokesman had confessed his fears which lie in much the same area.

"We are frightened by what seems to be a steady and continuing growth in the popularity of witchcraft and devil worship, and it is especially frightening to realize that it is attracting young people."

The threat posed by misguided involvement with the less savory aspects of the supernatural should not be under-rated. It is very serious. In England, there has been a positive step taken in dealing with this unexpected, but nonetheless critical, problem. An ecumenical commission of Anglicans and Roman Catholics acknowledged the influx of satanists and occultists among the young people in their areas. They recommended that each diocese appoint an official exorcist capable of driving out demons.

The Reverend Thomas Wills told an Anglican synod, "This is a problem that the church has not met for the past two hundred years ... the supernatural is gaining ascendancy ... more and more people are dabbling in fortune telling, séances held in the home, witchcraft and Black Magic."

There is really only one way to combat those who would mislead the ignorant, and that is to supply as many people as possible with a strong dose of honest information. They must be told what is already known about the supernatural. There are two groups that should rise to this challenge — the psychic organizations and the churches.

A California preacher, Reverend Morris Cerullo, formed the world's first anti-occult mobile unit to tour 45 American cities in the summer of 1972. He planned to use the "Witchmobile," stocked with more than a hundred occult articles, to fight increased preoccupation with the occult. Reverend Cerullo is particularly concerned about youngsters.

In the past, churches have maintained that the matter of spiritual life after physical death was beyong human understanding. We were taught that this was a subject largely dependent upon the individual's faith. This is simply not an adequate answer — it is a cop-out. There are those on the astral plane who do not meet the standard qualifications for long-term suffering. Despite having led exemplary lives upon earth, many of these spirits are obviously in great need of assistance.

Saying that humans cannot understand places the entire field of the supernatural beyond the comprehension of the church leaders themselves. It also discourages people from asking questions that they feel are very important to themselves and their families. It is not too surprising, therefore, to discover now that some of these individuals have begun looking elsewhere for the answers. This is how they get into trouble.

The frequent failure of exorcism indicates a lack of control, a rather frightening lack, over spiritual matters by those very people who purport to be able to advise us about our crucial spiritual destinies. When supernatural phenomena occur, clergymen are often the first to be called. They are asked for assistance, explanation and guidance. Up until now, they have not established much of a record for rendering the required help.

Even today, many evangelicals and fundamentalists regard every single aspect of the occult as a threatening and demonic danger. They refuse to allow that the world of the supernatural might have something of value, something to teach us. With such a negative attitude, they cannot be expected to cope with the rising interest now found in Canada.

It might be advisable for our modern clerics to jointly promote the training of young people with natural psychic abilities. This might clarify our relationship with that strange world just beyond us.

I am not the only individual who feels that the church, in general, lacks certain qualifications for fusing the link of understanding between living humans and those of the spirit world. My complaint is neither new nor unique despite its relevancy to contemporary problems.

In 1949, a copper miner named James Kidd disappeared somewhere in the vicinity of Globe in Arizona. After the required length of time had elapsed, he was declared legally dead and his will came up for probate.

James Kidd left an interesting and highly controversial will. It specifically designated that his entire estate was to be used in research "for some scientific proof of a soul of a human individual which leaves the body at death."

You would think that the stipulation requiring the production of scientific proof would limit the number of possible claimants. Perhaps it did, but one hundred and thirty-nine people and groups came forward asserting that they could provide the desired proof.

In 1967, Judge Robert Myers studied all the claims on Kidd's estate. He ruled that the Barrow Neurological Institute was the best qualified of the applicants to conduct research on the existence of a human soul.

The Supreme Court disagreed with Judge Myers' decision. After extended argument, they overturned his ruling. They held that the American Society for Psychical Research possessed better qualifications. This society, based in New York with affiliated groups throughout the United States, is now entrusted with the task.

In 1970, Joseph Bayley published *What About Horoscopes*. In it, he joined those who question the Church's ability to provide us with the much-needed guidance regarding the supernatural.

"To many people," Bayley said, "Today's church seems impotent because it is identified with the problems it should be solving."

Once again, the onus is on eliminating the past secrecy and probing deeper for answers.

I AM CURIOUS

In May of 1901, Ralph D. Blumenfeld, London *Daily Mail* correspondent was quoted in a rather unusual statement.

"I am not a believer in ghosts, nor am I a disbeliever. I am not a spiritualist, nor am I a skeptic. I simply don't know. But I am curious."

This opinion was considered unique at the time, but it is being expressed much more frequently today. It generally includes a rider or addition that goes something like; "And I want to know because it seems important. I feel it is something we should at least try to understand."

It would be reassuring to know that the clergy actively share the increased interest and desire to learn. Some of them certainly do. Those individuals who have personally or indirectly become involved in supernatural phenomena admit to a woeful lack of real knowledge in these matters. It is candid men such as these who accurately reflect the times. They recognize the desperate need to modernize and learn through study and experience. They, too, want to know.

Religion has been involved, directly or indirectly, in enough representational phenomena to warrant an attempt to find a bridge between the two fields of knowledge. There is a definite need for positive leadership, and one hopes the clergy may prove willing to undertake the responsibility. We have some of the answers. With a concentrated effort, perhaps we can learn more. It is high time that ghosts and other manifestations ceased to be considered fearful and evil things. They may not be a part of life as we now know it, but they certainly are a part of existence.

Considering all the reports about supernatural phenomena that we have had over the years and are still receiving regularly today, one point becomes increasingly evident. And I cannot stress the importance of this conclusion enough. There are many things beyond our limited understanding at present, and it is about time we applied ourselves in order to find out more about them.

People who don't even want to believe in such things as ghosts have admitted having experiences involving manifestations. Some of the incidents were amusing; others were quite frightening. But our theological teachings to date simply do not account for, or allow, another subworld in which souls or spirits wander aimlessly about for varying periods of time. These apparitions or shades appear to receive no guidance from a higher power as some of us have been led to expect. They are just there, and nobody seems to care.

Truly, the realm of ghosts stands exposed as a mixed limbo into which both evil and good have been flung apparently at random. The consistency that might indicate that this is a planned state or developmental stage of transition is lacking. And, since it is becoming more and more difficult to deny the existence of ghosts, the logical thing is to make room for them and learn to cope with their persistent demands.

Chapter Fourteen

PRAIRIE PHENOMENA

WHO'S BEEN SLEEPING IN MY ROOM?

One of the best-behaved and least offensive modern Canadian ghosts lives in Kindersley, Saskatchewan. He seems only to want to be in or near a specific room in which he may once have lived for a short time.

Since the Kindersley house is only about eight or nine years old, this fellow appears to be a relatively recent entry into the world of ghosts. If he were from another period of history, his interest would not likely be confined to that one specific room in the house. And no other structure has ever occupied that site.

The strange spirit first appeared at the Sprague (not their real name) home during the Christmas holidays of 1968. On that occasion, he inadvertently startled one of the Sprague girls. She was sleeping in what this spirit obviously considers to be "his" room. She awakened to find an unidentified man sitting calmly on the end of the bed and staring fixedly at her. He was dressed in black and wore a black, brimmed hat. A cat that had been sharing the room with the girl that night left with dispatch and refused to come back.

The ghost left without saying or doing anything. Showing more bravery than I could have mustered under similar circumstances, the young lady did not panic. She just went back to sleep. But then this girl had an advantage over most of us; she believed very strongly in the supernatural and accepted the presence of ghosts without hesitation.

The uninvited visitor, still dressed all in black, appeared again. This time he was seen by a male guest who had also been assigned to the same room. Early one morning, Mrs. Sprague's son went to wake their guest. The sleepy guest became aware of a man about six feet in height standing beside the boy inside the doorway. Later he mentioned the incident at the breakfast table, only to be greeted by a strange silence as his hosts exchanged glances.

A quick poll showed that only the boy had been anywhere near that area so early in the morning. And none of the other Spragues came even close to fitting the description of the spirit. The boy had been totally unaware of the stranger being beside him in the doorway. He had seen nothing.

When questioned, all the flustered guest could remember was that the ghost, or whatever it was, had possessed especially long arms. And, since he had been lying in bed at the time, his estimate of the stranger's height might not be quite accurate.

In 1969, yet another night-time appearance took place in the home of the Sprague family. This time, however, the man no longer wore his hat. He had grey hair, cut in what was later described as a "long brush cut," and moved silently from the side of the bed to its foot. And, after just standing there staring for a moment or two, he simply vanished.

The woman sleeping in the room that night left on the heels of the departing ghost. She slept elsewhere until dawn and later claimed that the ghost had touched her.

This ghost is unusual in a number of ways. Generally we hear only those tales which involve people who are having trouble with difficult spirits. This, in turn, has led to the widely accepted belief that all ghosts are annoying.

But this spirit has made no requests or demands. Nor has it really bothered any members of the family. Some guests have been surprised, but the Spragues' daily routine has been undisturbed. The visits are restricted to night and the early morning hours, and are only of brief duration. No exorcisms have been tried; nor are any being contemplated for the future.

Because of the lack of violent activity, fear and journalistic "color", this story did not reach the press or the public. There was no need to tell anyone about it. And so it is with a great many ghost stories. Spirits are a lot like teenagers in that the reading public hear only about the more troublesome ones.

Well, there is at least one quiet ghost, settled and more or less accepted, in a relatively new Saskatchewan home. Probably there are a lot more of them who are equally inoffensive, scattered throughout the provinces of Canada.

Not that ghosts make ideal housepets. Far from it! This story is included merely to indicate that they are not all that easy to categorize — spirits do not all look and act like escapees from the late-night horror shows on television. They are individuals, just like you and me, and should be treated accordingly.

THE COUNTERFEITERS

Now we come to a less recent haunting, one that was caused entirely by ordinary living humans.

For many years, a deserted house stood upon the banks of the Assiniboine River in Winnipeg, Manitoba. Weeds and tall unkempt grass filled the yard, and the nearest neighbors were more than a city block away.

A reporter describing this building wrote, 'It was a three-storey house with dormer windows on the third floor. The panes were smashed and the slats of the green shutters were broken. The shutters themselves were swaying to and fro on sagging hinges with every vagrant breeze that blew."

It was a classic setting for a haunting — isolated and rundown.

Imaginative youngsters and neighbors living close to this building shared the firm belief that one or more ghosts had taken up permanent residence in the empty house. They took care to stay well away from the area.

Various stories were told to account for the alleged haunting, some amusing and others quite bizarre and inventive. The tale most commonly accepted as genuine was that the eldest son of the owner had broken his neck in a fall down the basement stairs. His spirit was said to be still active and most unfriendly towards people who tried to enter the old house.

Police action was finally required to disprove the neighborhood theory. And it left a lot of people feeling very foolish indeed.

While the owner of this property, a well-known Winnipeg businessman, was on an extended European trip, a group of counterfeiters had stumbled across the deserted house. It was ideal for their purposes. And it was these men who were directly responsible for giving the house a reputation for being haunted. They invented the story of an angry and vengeful spirit and encouraged the belief whenever possible.

A cave was cut into one of the basement walls. Whenever unwelcome intruders appeared, the clever criminals would cover themselves with ordinary sheets outlined with phosphorus. Then, they would leap out from the cave and wave their arms wildly about in the air, moaning and groaning as they moved! No one encountering such "spectres" would be likely to return in the near future.

It took only a very short time for these men to turn their hideout into an area left entirely alone by the local residents. They came and went as they pleased.

The Winnipeg police eventually rounded up the counterfeiters, discovered the outlined sheets and illicit equipment, and effectively ended this particular haunting. The house was later torn down, and the site is now occupied by a school.

A CALL FOR HELP

Sometimes an event involves mental telepathy and this can be just as eerie and as difficult to explain as seeing a ghost.

An example of mental telepathy took place in 1940 on a prosperous farm near Prince Albert, Saskatchewan. The farmhouse was old and situated at least a mile from the nearest neighbor. The Erlichs were a devout family and belonged to an Evangelical sect. The one blot on their otherwise comfortable existence was the fact that their twenty-year-old son, Peter, was completely paralyzed. As well as being unable to move his arms or legs, Peter could not speak. He was capable of making animal-like noises which, combined with his facial expressions, were understood by his family.

One warm, July morning, the entire family went to church a few miles away, leaving Peter in the care of a young house guest, Margaret Bateman. After checking to see that Peter was safely in his bed, Margaret went out into the garden to pick raspberries. Half-an hour later, as she stood in the garden, she heard her name called clearly, in a musical voice. "Margaret ! Margaret !"

Knowing she was completely alone on the farm, except for Peter, she was startled. But she decided that some member of the family must have come back early. She went to the house to find out who had returned. There was no sign of the Erlich car, nor was there anybody around the house.

Margaret went in to look at Peter. Somehow, he had fallen out of bed and was lying with his face pressed down into the carpet. He could scarcely breathe and yet he could not move to turn himself over. His face was discolored and he was in distress. Margaret turned him over and made him as comfortable as she could on the floor until the family returned to help lift him back to his bed.

Although she could not explain the beautiful voice, Margaret felt that somehow, Peter had called for help and that she had heard him.

CHILD AT THE CROSSROADS

Elinor Telsky's family lived for a while in a small, closely knit, farm community near Yorkton in Saskatchewan. It was a large family effectively headed by her grandfather, a very religious individual who took his responsibilities seriously and was highly respected by all the neighbors

Strange things frequently happened at the crossroads near Elinor's home and these are the details of two of the more interesting and memorable occasions.

One of the most common occurrences at the crossroads involved the spirit of a small girl, about three or four years of age. This child would appear, unattended and apparently unsupervised, along the side of the road. People used to worry about the little girl as she wandered about through the tall weeds all by herself. No one knew whose child she might be or from where she had come. She would vanish whenever the local residents, concerned about her safety, tried to approach her for questioning.

As the years went by, the child kept returning to the edge of the road with no apparent signs of natural aging. The people in the community came to accept her presence. No explanation was ever found to account for this child's sporadic appearances.

The tiny girl's wanderings were not the sole reason for considering the area near the crossroads to be unusual. Other things happened too.

Every year, just before Easter, the local Greek Orthodox Church held a very special service. One member of each family took a bottle of water to the church to have it blessed. The holy water was later sprinkled about the local homes to prevent difficulties during the coming year. The water was also considered to possess curative powers and could be used internally in times of family sickness.

During the year in which we are interested, the service for blessing the water was to be held quite late at night. This was necessary. The minister had to visit several other churches in the area, and it would be after eleven o'clock by the time he reached the isolated community near Yorkton.

Shortly before ten in the evening, men started to assemble at the crossroads. It was a natural meeting place. They came from the various nearby farms and would walk in small friendly groups for the mile and a half distance to the church.

Elinor's grandfather was with a friend and they were just starting out along the road when he spotted a faint light in the distance. He slowed down, saying;

"That must be Arthur, late as usual. I rather thought he might join us this evening. Let's wait for him to catch up."

The two men stood quietly talking and waiting for their friend. They were both carrying their water jars, and Elinor's grandfather lit his long curved pipe as they chatted about weather and crops.

The light grew brighter as it approached them from across the fields. One of the men called out impatiently;

"Hurry up, Arthur! We don't want to be late and we've quite a long walk ahead of us. Most of the others have already left, but we can all use the same lantern if you'll just hurry up."

There was no answer, but neither of the men thought much about it at the time. There were fresh water springs running through the area and they just assumed that the sound of Arthur's footsteps and the gurgle of running water had prevented their friend from hearing their urging for haste.

Nearer and nearer came the bobbing lantern.

Elinor's grandfather and his friend got ready to greet Arthur. But, they both stopped abruptly in mid-sentence. The lantern came right up to where they were standing and passed between them. Nobody was carrying it! It was just bobbing along through the air at the correct carrying level all by itself. They knew that such a thing was not possible, or even natural, but both of them saw exactly the same thing.

The two friends stared in shocked and silent amazement as the strange lantern went on its way in the direction of the church. When it reached the fence, they could hear the distinctive sound of barbed wire being pushed aside to allow passage through the strands. The wires spread wide enough to allow a grown man to pass through the space and then the lantern appeared, still bobbing, on the other side of the fencing.

The men stood there, utterly speechless, for a few minutes. They watched as the lantern's glow gradually faded away in the direction of the evening service. Then, temporarily forgetting about the annual blessing and still clutching their water jugs, they headed for the closest residence.

Elinor met her grandfather and his friend at the door of her home. The two older men were pale and obviously shaken. At first, they refused to discuss what had happened to upset them, but they later told the family about the peculiar events out by the road.

Then, reminded of their responsibility to obtain the annual blessing on the water, the two men pondered the strange bobbing lantern as they bravely resumed the long walk to the church.

The next day, it was learned that Arthur had, indeed, planned to walk along with the others to the evening service. He had been unable to go at the last moment. He stated firmly that he had not even left the house that night.

The other two men were left to wonder who or what had carried that lantern from the direction of Arthur's farm towards the evening service at the church.

THE TABER SPOOK

For fiction writers, the world of the supernatural offers a limitless supply of material in which they can let their vivid imaginations have full reign. The many adaptations and variations of a simple haunting available to a truly creative writer are endless.

Sometimes the result of such innovation is a classic horror story, along the lines of the late Edgar Allan Poe's work. Even Shakespeare used ghosts in his tragedies and historical plays.

But occasionally a talented author with a touch of whimsy can create a totally harmless, thoroughly enjoyable piece of prose. Such an article appeared in *The Taber Times* of Alberta in 1968. It was written by H. George Meyer, publisher and editor of that newspaper and he has very kindly given his permission to pass it along. I include it here to show that ghosts do not have to be scarey or controversial subjects. Sometimes, at least in fiction, they can be funny.

"A strange thing happened to me the other night.

I was in the back yard in my nightshirt looking for the family cat. He had just had another round with Kent Westhora's cat, and our delicate feline wound up the vanquished again ... as usual. At least, judging by the sounds of battle, it was my guess Benjy needed rescuing.

As I wandered about in the black of the night — the street lights weren't even on — and called quietly: 'Come Benjy! Come, boy!', I suddenly heard a low, 'Woo-o-o-o-o'.

'Aha,' I thought to myself. 'Benjy is mortally wounded, because that's not the sound of any ordinary, healthy cat.' I continued the search more diligently after that, and as I rounded the corner of the garage, I came face to face with a glowing, misty, white form in the inky blackness. Naturally, I was a little more than mildly surprised, and in a highpitched, shaky voice, I asked, 'Who the Sam Hill are you and what do you want?"

'I'm a harmless spook,' came the reply, 'and, by Jove, old chap, I'm afraid I've become hopelessly lost.'

Noting the very British accent, I ventured: 'Well, I'm not accustomed to meeting lost spooks, but perhaps I can be of some help. Would you be from England, by chance?'

'Why ... yes!' came the spirit's startled reply. 'But, for the life of me, I jolly well can't guess how you could ever know that. But tell me,' he went on, as he carefully studied my nightshirt in the glow of his own reflection, 'Are you a spook, too?'

'No, I'm just a half-asleep mortal looking for a lost cat,' I said.

'Oh, look no further,' said the spook. 'He's safe and sound up on the roof of your house. Made it in one leap, too ... after he saw me.'

'Well, at least the cat is found,' I commented, 'but you are still lost. Now, where do you want to be?'

'Actually, I've got an appointment to haunt the cellar of Windsor Castle tonight, but I must have made a wrong turn somewhere. Tell me, where am I?'

When I advised him he was in Taber, Canada, he was quite astonished to find out he had drifted so far off course. I told him which way was east, and he was about to leave when, as an after-thought, he said, 'By the way, old chap, can I return your kindness in any way?'

'Well,' I replied, with barely a second's hesitation, 'How about letting me take your picture? Nobody will believe that I was talking to you if I can't print a picture of you in *The Times* to prove it.'

'Capital idea!' exclaimed the ghost, 'but you'll have to use a flash unit. You see, in spite of my glow, I wouldn't show up on a film without a flash exposure.'

'That's fine,' I said. 'I have a flash gun attached to my camera, and it's right here in the car.'

I took the camera out, set it carefully, sighted up the smiling spook and clicked the shutter. But wouldn't you know? The flash didn't work. I had neglected to recharge the battery that day.

The spook, of course, was late for his appointment and couldn't stay around long enough for me to recharge the battery.

So, that is the sad story: a photogenic ghost and a battery too run down to make the flash gun work.

Just another case of 'The spirit was willing, but the flash was weak.' "

Although the incident in Taber was fictional, Mr. Meyer has quite skillfully utilized many of the factors consistently found in genuine hauntings. His cat flees from the ghost in complete panic, just as so many animals fear and try to avoid contact with the supernatural. The sleepy mortal himself is temporarily knocked off balance by his first sight of the spirit. The ghost is able to cover great distances in a brief period of time, and there is the usual difficulty in getting some sort of tangible proof that the event occurred as reported.

This talented writer has, perhaps unknowingly, shown that he agrees with some modern ghost-hunters in their contention that all ghosts are not nasty. He epitomizes the wish of all of us, to be able to assist these confused spirits whenever possible. And, he weakens in only one spot. That is when he imports his ghost from Great Britain, instead of using a Canadian product !

TAPE-RECORDED SPIRITS

In the middle of January of 1963, Edmonton reported a strange and disturbing haunting. Investigators felt it might have been caused by a relatively mild-mannered poltergeist. Since there was no real personal violence and no small children were implicated in any way, this could be also have been a confused spirit trying in vain to communicate meaningfully with the living. One can make a fairly good case for either side of the argument.

It was winter when the Harold Sydora family of Edmonton first noticed that something was wrong. They began to hear unexplainable knockings and bangings. In the beginning, they attributed these odd noises to the age of their house. A lot of time was wasted while the Sydoras worried about faulty construction, wiring or plumbing connections.

Then there were the sounds of definite footsteps. Strange rapping sessions kept the family awake at night. These continued for a short period, and were followed by an uneasy silence. There was an almost tangible tension in the atmosphere. Then the noises resumed.

The Sydoras told their friends and neighbors about their disturbed nights, and tried to find someone who could advise them. The resultant flow of willing, interested, but unhelpful persons seemed to discourage the invisible thumper. The noises stopped again.

The peace lasted for almost a week, although one incident did occur during that period. Harry Sydora had the unsettling experience of waking up one night to discover his blanket being moved right up over his face! No one was near the bed at that time, and he certainly hadn't raised the blanket himself.

A member of the large family spoke for all the Sydoras when she said, "We have a feeling that the peace won't last."

The apprehension turned out to be quite justified. Later that same week, at four in the morning when everything was calm and quiet, the noisy troublemaker did return.

This turn of events came as a bad shock to the family despite the fact that they had been half-expecting it. It was also, ironically, a bit of a relief. Many people had begun to express disbelief in the story, and some had actually accused the Sydoras of trickery. It is bad enough to have some sort of manifestation operating in your home; it is far worse to be accused of having created the unusual situation for your own selfish purposes.

This time, however, there could be no doubt. Although all ten members of the family were asleep when the disturbance began, a tape-recorder had been placed in the house by an enterprising local reporter. It faithfully took down the entire performance from start to finish.

"Now, we've got it on tape," said Harry Sydora, "and it's here for anybody to hear."

First, there was a heavy pounding on the walls and ceilings, loud enough to arouse everyone in the household. The noises moved around, making it impossible to locate their source. It sounded almost as if someone or something was walking heavily about on the main floor of the three-storey house.

But no one slept on that floor. Nor was anyone even

near the area involved. Those members of the family who had been sleeping in the basement bedrooms fled to the upper floor. They remained together in a lighted room until dawn marked the end of the disturbance.

The people involved in this experience said that some of noises they heard were 'almost human."

Twenty-year-old Ann Sydora summed up the incident.

"The sound stopped for maybe four minutes, then it returned loud as ever for maybe another five minutes. It was quiet for a couple of days, but whatever-it-was sure made up for it tonight!"

The Sydoras were ready to vacate as soon as possible. They felt that they had endured a demonstration that should have proved to some of the unbelievers that there was something unnatural in their home. And, they had no intention of sharing already-crowded accommodations with a poltergeist.

Aged fifty at the time of this experience, Harry Sydora had been warned by several doctors that he must remain as calm as possible. They felt he was dangerously close to a nervous breakdown. He had, quite understandably, developed a severe case of insomnia during this trying period.

A minister was reported to have heard the mysterious knockings and rappings at the Sydora residence. If this is so, he may have tried to exorcise the noisy spirit. But there was no evidence of a successful exorcism at that time. The thing was not quelled in the least. Apparently the uninvited and unappreciated visitor was not suitably impressed by the rites held in his honor.

Several more banging sessions occurred and then, over a period of time, the noises began to fade away. The noisy exhibitionist eventually ceased his night-time performances. The Sydoras did not release any more stories about their problem.

"I was criticized for talking to the press," said Mr. Sydora. "But what could I do ? I needed help."

It will be interesting to see if the relative calm continues to exist in the old house. As mentioned earlier, poltergeists tend to be associated with people rather than with specific places. If this actually was a poltergeist, the mildness of its activities may have only been a prelude for noisier and more violent scenes.

On the other hand, the Sydoras may have encountered a ghost with some sort of motivation or purpose behind its peculiar noisy actions. It may have fulfilled its mission or it may be simply waiting in the house for a return engagement in Edmonton.

Chapter Fifteen

CONCLUSION

It would appear that, despite valiant and misguided attempts to cover up or rationalize supernatural incidents here in Canada, we still have unnatural occurrences. The various phenomena of poltergeists, ghostly returns from beyond the grave, and messages from the past and future continue to infiltrate our "modern" society.

Canadians are advancing steadily on many fronts. Our attention is not absorbed by indirect participation in a war, and many scientific, sociological and medical advancements have been credited to our present generation. As admirable and necessary as this progress may be, it should not be made at the expense of the North American folklore and belief in spirits.

There is much that we could learn from a full investigation of psychic phenomena. But, in order to do this, we must have the help of all witnesses to unnatural events. We need to make the study of the supernatural respectable so that all will be willing to participate. Those who deliberately or inadvertently hinder the detailed investigation of unusual incidents only slow down the work temporarily. Where there is a need and a desire to know and learn, people have always managed to obtain the information they required despite opposition.

Already, common characteristics are being found in many of the psychic cases. It should not be too long before a clear pattern emerges. And that is when we will be better able to understand such fascinating things as ghosts, poltergeists, forerunners and hindsight. This knowledge may have quite serious implications upon our present way of life. It might help to solve some of the recurrent questions concerning an afterlife.

Americans and Canadians share an inclination to neglect their rich spiritual heritage. By so doing, they minimize its importance in their daily lives. The tendency is to pretend that all supernatural manifestations are a thing of the past or, obversely, to accept blindly everything they are told about the various phenomena.

Unless they are confronted with a major incident which affects them personally, people associate ghost stories with strange tales told in whispers by their grandparents. And, even then, the common reaction is to deny the evidence of their own senses and to proclaim blandly that nothing unusual has happened. These people are as mistaken as those who swallow all sorts of strange material without proper consideration.

The folklore and legends that stem from a truly international mixture of races form the backbone and moral strength of the country itself. To pretend that unnatural phenomena did not exist in the past, and do not occur with similar regularity today, is to deny historical fact and precedent. It denies our children some of their rightful heritage. And, equally important, it also casts doubt upon the integrity of a great many Canadians who have encountered manifestations.

Some of the people in the preceding chapters may have been lying deliberately for personal reasons. Still others may have been honestly mistaken about the strange things that happened to them. But I doubt if you can convince yourself that they were *all* in error. There are too many consistencies in the stories from across the country, striking similarities that show supernatural manifestations to have a certain constancy and an almost predictable likeness of detail.

Ghosts have been with us since the days when only the Indians occupied this vast land. And they are still here creating confusion today. Rationalizations and semi-accurate justifications are not acceptable to the questioning Canadians of today. Nor is there any reason why they should be accepted. Ghosts do exist — and we would be wise to recognize this fact and to learn all that we can about the associated phenomena.

The June 19, 1972 edition of *Time* magazine summed up the hope for the future very well. It stated, "Perhaps, eventually, religion, science and magic could come mutually to respect and supplement one another. This is a fond vision, and one that is pinned to a fragile and perpetually unprovable faith; that the universe itself is a whole, with purpose and promise beneath the mystery."

BIBLIOGRAPHY

Bluenose Ghosts : Helen Creighton, Ryerson Press, 1957.

Exploring the Surnatural; R. S. Lambert, McClelland & Stewart, 1955.

50 Great Ghost Stories; edited by John Canning, Odhams Books Ltd., 1966.

Ghosts I have Known; Eileen Sonin, Clarke, Irwin & Co. Ltd., 1969.

The Lively Ghosts of Ireland; Hans Holzer, Bobbs-Merrill Co., Inc., 1967.

Mind Over Space; Nandor Fodor, Citadel Press, 1962.

Nominigan; Mary L. Northway, Brora Centre, Toronto, 1969.

Red Blood and Royal; Paul Bloomfield, 1965.

The Tom Thomson Mystery; W. T. Little; McGraw-Hill, 1970.

What About Horoscope; James Bayley, 1970.

Toronto Globe & Mail; Trailing the Ghosts in Britain, Nov. 6, 1963.

Toronto Daily Star; BOAC Ghost Tour, Gerry Hall.

Montreal Star; Johane Allison, St. Bruno.

Toronto Telegram; Scarborough house Ghost, Calvin Millar.

Halifax Mail-Star; Metal hoop and RCMP, Peter Outhit, 1960.

Chronicle-Herald; Country Harbor stories, Sarah M. Wilson, 1965.

London Free Press; Beatrice Simms story, Joe McClelland, 1969.

Reuter; Transplants in Chicago.

The Western Star; Maritime stories, Ray MacLeod, Newfoundland.

Toronto Globe & Mail; Oak Island, Nova Scotia, Lyndon Watkins.

Weekend Magazine; Oak Island, Nova Scotia, Kerry Ellard.

Time Magazine; The Occult, June 19, 1972.

Weekend Magazine; Gertrud in Brockville, Doyle Klyn.

Toronto Telegram; Old City Hall and Mackenzie House, John Clare.

Toronto Telegram; Mackenzie House, Andrew MacFarlane.

Montreal Gazette; Freda MacGachen, librarian.

Toronto Telegram; St. Catharines ghost, John Sharp, 1970.

Edmonton Journal; Sydora ghost, James Roebuck and Al Dahl, 1963.

Canadian Press; Keswick bloodstains, 1963.

Press Library; Vancouver.

Vancouver Sun; Hetty Frederickson ghost, Jess Odam & Michael Cobb.

Winnipeg Free Press; Counterfeiters, G. Lemieux. Ruth Buggey, librarian.

Taber Times; Taber Spook, H. G. Meyer, 1968, Taber, Alberta.

The Northern Light; Teazer story and phantom ship of Bay Chaleur, Frank Mersereau, Bathurst, New Brunswick.

Vancouver Sun Province; Oak Bay ghosts, Frank Curtin.

Victoria Daily Times; Oak Bay ghosts.

Victoria Daily Colonist; Oak Bay ghosts.

Whitby World; Maritime grave, Judy Durkee.

Dauphin Herald; Shirley McCallum, Dauphin, Manitoba.

Western Advertiser; Louise Hunt, Mary Fairfield, Penticton, B.C.

Windsor Star; Frances Curry, librarian.

Fundy Printers; Fred A. Hatfield, Digby, N.S.

Montreal Star; C. M. Lapointe, librarian.

Peace River Block News; Kevan Van Herd, Dawson Creek, B.C.

Toronto Globe & Mail; Leone Kirkwood.

Toronto Globe & Mail; Tom Thomson ghost, Lesma Hossack, 1970.

Toronto Globe & Mail; Ackerman story.

CANADIAN
Paperback Originals by Canadian Authors

FICTION

☐ **THE LOVELIEST AND THE BEST** by Angela O'Connell. An adult love story for the men and women who lived World War II . . (78621—$1.50)

☐ **BACKROOM BOYS AND GIRLS** by John Philip Maclean. A novel that raises basic questions about Canadian politicians—and sex. (78622—$1.50)

☐ **THE QUEERS OF NEW YORK** by Leo Orenstein. A novel of the homosexual underworld. . . . .(78262—$1.25)

☐ **RIGHT NOW WOULD BE A GOOD TIME TO CUT MY THROAT** by Paul Fulford. A bawdy sailor adrift in Toronto publishing circles. (78252—$1.25)

☐ **FESTIVAL** by Bryan Hay. A modern novel which reveals the rip-off of drug-crazy kids by music festival promoters . . . .(77536—.95)

☐ **THE GHOSTS OF WAR** by Michael Foxwell. A love story which reveals the after-effects of war. . . . .(78644—$1.50)

☐ **GOD AND MRS. SULLIVAN**—Joy Carroll. The love affairs of a beautiful society woman with too much money . . . . .(78658—$1.50)

☐ **DADDY'S DARLING DAUGHTER**—William Thomas. A shocking novel of today's children and their life-style . . . .(78740—$1.50)

☐ **WILD INHERITANCE**—Robert Thurman. The gripping story of one family's struggle for survival—and success . . . .(78738—$1.50)

☐ **LOVE AFFAIR**—Earl Knickerbocker. The bitter-sweet romance of two young schoolteachers. . . . .(78744—$1.50)

☐ **THE LAST CANADIAN**—William Heine. A terrifying look at the future. (78743—$1.50)

SIMON & SCHUSTER of Canada Ltd.
330 Steelcase Road, Markham, Ontario

Please send me the POCKET BOOKS I have checked above. I am enclosing
$. . . . .(check or money order—no currency or C.O.D.'s. Please include the list price plus 25 cents to cover handling and mailing costs.)

Name . . . .

Address . . . .

City . . . . Province . . . . Zone . . . .

CANADIAN Paperback Originals by Canadian Authors

NONFICTION

☐ **WHY WEAR GLASSES?** by Dr. B. J. Slatt & Dr. H. A. Stein. A layman's guide to eye problems and the new soft contact lens.
(78565—$2.50)

☐ **THE SUMMER OLYMPIC GAMES** by Jock Carroll. Did you know Canada has won more than 250 medals in the Summer Olympics? A complete guide to the games & records. 100 photos of champions in action, with special attention to Canadian athletes. (78569—$2.50)

☐ Crosbie's **DICTIONARY OF PUNS** by John Crosbie. The world's punniest book and the world's first pun dictionary. .. (78217—$1.25)

☐ **PRO HOCKEY 74-75**—Jim Proudfoot. The hockey fan's annual Bible, by the Sports Editor of The Toronto Star .... (78750—$1.95)

☐ Percy Rowe's **TRAVEL GUIDE TO CANADA.** The first complete guide to every province & territory. Hotels, restaurants, museums, parks, campsites. .... (78596—$1.50)

☐ **SOME CANADIAN GHOSTS** by Sheila Hervey. An examination of strange occurrences and appearances across Canada. (78629—$1.50)

☐ **ALL QUIET ON THE RUSSIAN FRONT** by Kurt Stock. A German soldier, now a Canadian, reveals the horror of Russian P.O.W. camps.
(78630—$1.50)

☐ **THE HAPPY HAIRDRESSER** by Nicholas Loupos. A rollicking revelation of what Canadian women do and say when they let their hair down. .... (78654—$1.50)

☐ **DOWN THE ROAD**—Jock Carroll. Uninhibited talks with Marilyn Monroe and other famous sex symbols. Photos ..... (78739—$1.50)

C02/73

AMERICA'S
CHAMPION
Heloise
HOUSEKEEPER

HINTS FOR
WORKING WOMEN
ALL AROUND
THE HOUSE
HOUSEKEEPING
HINTS
KITCHEN HINTS
WORK & MONEY
SAVERS

Hundreds of helpful hints for easier, speedier, money-saving ways to accomplish every household task.

▼ **AT YOUR BOOKSTORE OR MAIL THE COUPON BELOW** ▼

RP 33/1

HOCKEY
BOOK BARGAINS